CW00481168

A BELL IN
BELLAPAIS

Echoes from a Cyprus Village

JOHN GUTHRIE

A Bell in Bellapais
Echoes from a Cyprus Village
written in 1985 by John Guthrie

Copyright © 2016 Deirdre Guthrie

First published 2016 by
MBW Publishing Enterprises
Markus Betzmeier-Wadams, Munich, Germany

Condition of Sale
This book is sold under the condition that it shall not, by any way of
trade or otherwise, be lent, re-sold, hired out or otherwise circulated
in any form of binding or cover other than that in which it is
published and without a similar condition including this condition
being imposed on the subsequent purchaser.

All rights reserved.
No part of this publication may be reproduced, stored in or
introduced into a retrieval system, or transmitted, in any form, or by
any means (electronic, mechanical, photocopying, recording or
otherwise) without the prior written permission of the publisher. Any
person who does any unauthorised act in relation to this publication
may be liable to criminal prosecution and civil claims for damages.

Cover, Design and Typeset by
Jay Wadams, Editor

Printed and bound in
Birkach, Germany

1st Edition

ISBN: 978-3-981-81229-9

For all our village friends.

CONTENTS

FOREWORD

The village of Bellapais in the northern hills of Cyprus is known to many people for its beauty and its ancient abbey, and to a large public through Lawrence Durrell's book 'Bitter Lemons', which vividly describes the village and the villagers nearly three decades ago.

We first came to Bellapais in 1951, bought a house and frequently returned, until 1962 when we permanently retired to the village in pursuit of peace and painting and musical composition. Now we find ourselves the only inhabitants remaining from those times. Perhaps an account of life within the village, as it was and as it is, may be worth the telling.

Politics have no place here. Much has been written about the troubled history of the island, past and recent, by those competent to do so. It is far beyond the scope and intentions of this simple story of the Bellapais we have known and loved for more than thirty years, and lived in continuously for more than twenty.

~ John and Vivian M. Guthrie.
1985.

Part I

JOHN GUTHRIE

PRELUDE

T he abbey bell is the clock and herald of the village, measuring the hours and days and months and seasons, summoning, proclaiming and giving news. It chimes for wakening in the mornings, peals for festivals and weddings in the afternoons, and sometimes slowly tolling in the evenings, tells of deaths.

CHIMES

The bell chimes for sunrise. The sun like a golden sovereign stands on the horizon, gilding the abbey and burnishing the bell as it swings in the honeyed light. The village sleeps and dreams, rocked in cradle rhythms of clocking time and heartbeat. The bell swings and rings. Chime and heartbeat separate uneasily as dreams dissolve. The village stirs and wakes to the realities of day.

Shutters open. Buckets clatter. Cocks crow. Donkeys bray. Boots clump on flagstones. Plates rattle. Women chatter. Children yawn. Soon the dissonances resolve as families disperse to work and school.

The village lies quiet and still, gleaming white and crystalline beneath the morning sun. Women sit at their thresholds spinning silk. In the fields the men tend trees, dig, plough or plant. Children play in the gardens. Doves wheel in the clear sky, suddenly disappearing as they turn against the sun, then

3

flashing white again. The olive trees beneath them join the game, shimmering from dark to silver in the breeze.

The measured hours pass. The sun hangs at the zenith.
The village dozes, drugged with heat, mesmerized by cicadas.
A fountain splashes in a shaded pool. Two dragonflies, one red, one blue, hover and circle above. In the cool deep water, goldfish lie motionless under yellow lotuses. It is the solstice of the day.

PEALS

The bell peals and peals in the afternoons. It peals for festivals and weddings, for fruition, reaping and harvesting, pealing and pealing in celebration of the sovereign sun. Boys on the abbey roof fly up, feet in the air, as they swing at the end of the bell rope.

Through the abbey door come bride and bridegroom, crowned with orange blossom. The wedding guests stream out behind them like a swarm of butterflies. Priest and fiddler lead the fluttering procession to the dowered house. The haloed pair sit enthroned to watch their feasting guests. Food vanishes from tables as the butterflies turn into locusts. Wine splashes from barrels into jugs and glasses. The fiddler taps his foot and starts to scrape. The guests leap up to dance.

Garlands of flowers hang on street doors. Water mumbles in mossy aqueducts. Vines intertwine and tangle with reddening pomegranates and fattening figs. Women stoop in the wheat fields. In swaying lines of faded blue and red they move into the trembling corn, swinging sickles, catching and embracing the swiftly toppling stalks. On the threshing grounds men sit on flint-shod boards pulled by nodding oxen, endlessly revolving. Clouds of gold dust drift above as the chaff is winnowed by the breeze.

Under the majestic sun, cypresses grow tall, thrusting like lances into the glowing sky among the headlong swifts. On the hillsides carobs blacken into ripeness, olives dance and shed their fruits.

Slowly the sun declines as summer relents to autumn. The last harvests are brought in across the stubbled fields. The sound of rattling stones in hollowing gourds foretells approaching winter.

THE BELL CHIMES

L ong years ago before it had lost its innocence, Bellapais in the foothills of the northern range of mountains, was surely the loveliest village in Cyprus, its name perfectly descriptive of its peaceful beauty, deriving from the Abbaye de la Belle Paix built in the time of the Crusades, round which the village grew.

Three people, John and Vivian and their small daughter Deirdre came upon it one unforgettable day some thirty years ago. The first glimpse of the village in the distance cast a spell upon them which was to change the course of their lives. Seeking escape from the sweltering heat in the little harbour town of Kyrenia where they were spending a holiday, they had driven into the nearby hills where perhaps it would be cooler. As they rounded a bend in the road the village came suddenly into view about half a mile away.

They stopped and gazed at it, a cluster of terracotta tiled and whitewashed houses huddled on a hillside and half hidden by trees and vines. At its foot stood the sturdy mass of the abbey, round which the village seemed to have grown as naturally as the vines and fruit trees in the gardens round the houses.

Above, rose limestone hills wooded with carob, pine and cypress. Beyond, the hills rolled on in craggy summits to distant perspectives lost in a shimmering haze. Below, the land fell away some eight hundred feet in a broad sweep of poppied fields, olive, almond and citrus trees, to the sea stretching like a sheet of pale blue silk to the coast of Anatolia forty miles away. A cool breeze stirred, bringing the scent of jasmine.

"It's too lovely to be true," said Vivian at last.
"Of course 'distance lends enchantment...'" John murmured.
"I wonder how a closer view will look."
"Let's go and see!" said Deirdre.

They drove on, entering the village through a narrow street lined by small white houses, their balconies banked with flowers, and gardens glimpsed through open doors. Outside the doors young women sat on kitchen chairs, backs turned modestly to the street, eyes lowered over sewing. An old woman with a basket of eggs on her arm passed by, and a few men riding donkeys. Dark-eyed children stood and waved, seeming to smile a welcome. The street came to an end as it opened suddenly into an ample square, studded here and there with shady trees beneath which a few old men sat dozing or sipping coffee. To one side the abbey loomed, honey-coloured in the light of late afternoon. The other sides of the square were bordered with small houses, an arcaded school house and a coffee shop. In the centre a tall slender cypress gently swayed above a well-kept flower garden.

"Well how do you like your closer view?" Vivian asked as they sat at a shaded table taking in the peaceful scene, and with it long cool drinks. Swifts and swallows circled in the clear sky. The silence was unbroken except for the drowsy drone of cicadas and an occasional squeak as an old man shifted in his chair. As the sun declined the honey colour of the abbey was deepening to gold.

"I like it better still," said John.

No one took notice of the three strangers, except a child who shyly offered Deirdre a handful of crumpled flowers, and the proprietor of the coffee shop, Dimitri, who ambled across the square bringing more cold beer unasked and lingered for a moment to say that it was 'on the house'.

"It is too lovely to be true," said Vivian again.
"I'd say it's lovely and it's also true," said John.
"Let's stay forever here," said Deirdre.

A few weeks of their holiday remained. All three agreed to spend them in the village, to explore it and find the 'feel' of it among the villagers. They rented a house near the abbey square. It wasn't very grand - three small rooms and an empty little kitchen. There was no bath, but the owner rigged up a shower beneath the stair. A petrol tin with holes pierced in the bottom and filled with buckets of tepid water served very well. They ate the simple food of the village, home baked bread, olives, eggs, dried beans and sometimes a roast of lamb, and followed the leisurely rhythms of village life. On the first morning they went to see the abbey and were greeted there by Costas Kollis the custodian, a stocky energetic figure with a sharp eye, an inquisitive well stored mind and a ready smile.

"I'll have to charge you the entrance fee this once," he said, "but as you're staying in the village you'll be welcome to come freely as often as you like. Let me take you round and tell you a little bit about it."

The abbey, founded late in the twelfth century by Augustinian Canons, built in the French Gothic style by the Lusignans who at that time ruled the island, and richly endowed from time to time by the kings of Jerusalem, had flourished for two centuries. Disagreements then arose between the monks and their superiors. (It is recorded that many of the brethren, breaking their vows of chastity, had taken wives). The monks fell out of favour, lost their patronage and their endowments, and the abbey already in decay, had slowly crumbled into ruin, though much remained in solid preservation.

The massive structure stood on a rocky escarpment, the edge of which fell sheer for a hundred feet, providing formidable protection and a commanding view from the refectory windows looking down upon the fields and orchards steeply sloping to the sea. The huge high-vaulted refectory reflecting the generosity of kings to the monks while still obedient to their vows, gave onto a cloister open to the sky, on all sides enclosed by decorated Gothic arches. In the middle of the grass lawn which carpeted the enclosure stood four tall cypresses.

"I planted those myself more than twenty years ago," said Costas, "and all this too," he added as he led the way from the cloister through a garden of trees and shrubs and flowers, to the church, the oldest part of the abbey and still intact. The broad square nave was austere and dark. Solid arches on either side gave support to the ancient dome blackened by smoke from countless candles. Beneath it the floor was bare except for wooden sedilias along the walls. The only relief from severity was the iconostasis in the chancel which glowed with mellow icons. For six centuries, all here had endured with little change, and in this church all the village services were still held. In the belfry above the nave, the big bell softly sounded its rich overtones and undertones as it swayed gently in the breeze.

There was much more to be explored on frequent further visits, the kitchen, cellarium and crypt, the chapter house where the monks had sat each morning on the still-existing stone seats round the walls, to be instructed by the Abbot, and above the chapter house, all that remained of the lofty dormitory.

Other mornings were spent exploring the narrow cobbled streets, discovering old olive presses, donkey stables and the few small shops, standing to watch old women deftly spinning silk as they sat absorbed outside front doors, peeping into gardens where the younger women baked bread in beehive ovens, or wandering in the surrounding fields and olive groves where Vivian might sit and paint while John and Deirdre went off on some small expedition, perhaps to join the water wardens on their irrigation rounds. At the end of the morning all three would scramble up the hillside to look down on the village clustered round its mother abbey, and listen to the small sounds drifting up to them till the midday heat drove them to siesta.

In the evenings they went to the abbey square to sit with their new-found friends, Dimitri and Costas Kollis, or just to watch the old men at their tric-trac boards, till it was cool enough to go to bed and hope for sleep.

Soon the 'feel' of the village was so familiar that a clock was hardly needed. Each day the hours were measured by the natural village sounds. Early morning was announced by the first cock crow, the creak of opening shutters, the clatter of plates and buckets, the clump of heavy boots on flagstones. A little later the clip-clop of donkeys' hooves on cobbles told that the men were riding away to the fields. Then silence for a while till clucking hens and gobble-gobble turkeys gathered to be fed. By mid-morning the sounds of squeaking spindles threaded with the shriller sounds of children's voices calling in the gardens, merged with the deeper undercurrent of water rushing and gurgling in irrigation channels. In the afternoons the village dozed, anaesthetized by cicadas, till early evening when the houses came to life again with busy kitchen sounds as suppers were prepared, and children on nearby balconies intoned their lessons for next day. The men returned, as hungry as their braying donkeys. Plates rattled once again. Voices rose and subsided into yawns. An hour after sunset the village was asleep to the lullaby of Skops owls calling from garden to garden in the still night air.

The abbey bell measuring the larger intervals of the days, chimed according to custom or occasion. On Sundays it rang insistently for the morning service till the church was filled and cantors quavering voices rose and fell in the archaic cadences of plainsong.

The spell the village had cast when first it had beckoned in the distance, held the three strangers more firmly captive each day within it. But all too soon they would have to leave.

One afternoon as they were sitting over coffee in the square, Costas Kollis came up to them. "There's a house for sale," he said "why don't you come and look at it?"

Houses were rarely put up for sale in those days. They were kept for bridal dowries. Since a young woman had to provide the house and furniture when she married, and as she seldom had the means to do so, her parents usually gave their first-born daughter their own house, adding another bedroom for themselves.

"But we already have a house in Scotland." said John "My wife doesn't have to provide me with another. Deirdre is only ten and as far as I'm aware has no immediate marriage plans. And any way we'll be off in a week or two and may never come back."
"Well just come and look at it. I'm sure you'll like the view."

They had nothing better to do, so they walked with Costas up the street to the top of the village where it ended on the hillside. On the crags above, forested, medieval and remote, the only sign of life was a herd of tinkling goats. Costas opened a broken wicket gate and led through a garden of rank weeds and stunted citrus trees, bounded on one side by a crumbling wall and on the other by a tumbling cliff.

The house was a neglected ruin. The flat roof was cracked and far from rain-proof. The walls were of rubble which showed through a veneer of flaking plaster. Pushing aside the front door hanging at an angle from one rusty hinge, they entered with little enthusiasm to inspect the rooms. Upstairs there were two, a living room and a small bedroom separated from it by a flimsy lath and plaster wall. At one end of the living room there was an open fireplace which had evidently been used for cooking. Downstairs, if it could be so described since there was no connecting stair, there was the traditional donkey stable with a stone byre along one wall, and another which had been used for junk and fodder. All the rooms were floored with earth and straw. There was no kitchen, no bathroom, no lavatory, no plumbing, no water, no electricity and no furniture. The house for sale was hardly a 'desirable residence'.

"But you haven't looked at the view," said Costas a little petulantly. John and Vivian stepped warily across the shaky upstairs floor and looked out through the broken windows. There lay the village below them, a close pattern of tiles and small white houses, leafy with vines and fruit trees. Beyond, dominating all in full clear view stood the abbey, and across the sea the misty coast of Anatolia. Costas with an inscrutable smile took Deirdre out to the garden, leaving John and Vivian to stand and look.

Vivian was the first to break the silence.

"What a view! How lovely it would be to have a house in Bellapais."
"Well we could if we really wanted to."
"But it's much too far from where we'll be for most of the rest of our lives."
"We could come on holidays and retire here when we're old."
"No, it's just a dream."
"Why not say 'yes' because it is a dream? We'll never find another like it. Dreams soon fade into regrets unless you seize

them on the impulse. You have to believe in them and make them real."

"It's too late now to think of dreams. There's no time left to find a house."

"But we've just found it. We're standing in it now. Let's buy it."

"Oh do wake up. How could we ever live in this collapsing ruin?"

"We couldn't in its present state of course. But we could rebuild it and shape it to our needs. The foundations seem solid and there's plenty of room to extend into the garden. It wouldn't cost us much, the owner surely must be eager to be rid of it. What do you say?"

Vivian looked again at the shabby walls, the wood worm riddled beams, the unsafe floor, the peeling plaster and the rotten window frames. She was silent for some minutes, till she turned once more to the view. Then with a sigh and a sudden smile she said, "All right. Let's have it."

The next day they bought it.

Costas found the owner and her husband in the nearby village to which some years ago they had departed, and brought them hot-foot to Bellapais. The owner of the house, a plump young woman in her prime, was laughing and talking excitedly with Costas as John and Vivian approached. Then, evidently realizing that these were the prospective buyers, her expression changed into a tragic mask, the meaning of which seemed plain. "How could you rob a poor young mother and her starving children of their home?" In her arms she held a protesting but well-nourished child, Two others clutching at her skirt, stared with wide accusing eyes at John and Vivian. Clearly this had all been well rehearsed though hardly worth the trouble. Perhaps the 'woebegone' young mother was unaware that her customers knew that she herself had abandoned her house to ruination years ago. Still it was a useful warning of unexpectedly hard bargaining ahead.

Costas then introduced her husband, a tall lean man with stony eyes, tight lips and a joyless smile, who was to talk business on his wife's behalf. John and Vivian looked at him with some disquiet, then hopefully at the cheerful Costas his confident middleman. Even with his help the talk was obviously going to be anything but cosy. The grieving owner, and her children crying inconsolably, no doubt still on cue, then left the four to their deliberations.

They sat down in the square at a table beneath a shady tree and ordered four cold beers. Since the owner's husband spoke no English and John and Vivian no Greek, Costas agreed to act as their interpreter and go-between. He would be very happy to help his good friends to reach an amicable agreement, he said, as he raised his glass and beamed at the three expectant but impassive faces. John and Vivian glanced at the owner's husband. If he too was feeling amicable he betrayed no noticeable signs of it. Nor, it must be said, did any show of affability occur to John and Vivian.

The smile on Costas's face faded a little as he continued his preamble. This was a unique occasion, he observed. It was the first time a village house had ever been offered for sale to a foreigner, and happily as his client had just remarked to him, the house, fitting the occasion, was itself unique. Costas hurried on. John and Vivian were to be congratulated for having so wisely decided to buy the house which had enchanted them even at first sight. Obviously they knew a good thing when they saw it. Where else in the world would they find a house with such a view? And how lucky indeed they were that the owner was willing to let them have it. For her of course it was a heart-break. She had decided to part with it only because she was much in need of money.
As Costas paused to translate this to his client, and listen to his next instructions, John received a sharp nudge in the ribs. "Two corrections," Vivian whispered. "We've made no decision yet,

and the house does not enchant us. Ask Costas to make that clear to Hard-eyes."

"Let's not go so fast," said John as Costas was about to continue, doubtless with further eulogies. "We've not yet made up our minds to buy the property. The view is certainly enchanting But the so-called house is not. Your client has described it as 'unique'. We'd call it something else."

The message was delivered and discussed. The hard-eyes turned to flint. Costas, somewhat subdued but doing his best as go-between returned to the defence. Well, what did they have to say about the house, his friend would like to know?

"Plenty," said John. "It's a wreck. You can see daylight through the roof, the walls are crumbling, the timbers are all rotten, and it lacks even the most rudimentary necessities, unless you count the byre in the donkey stable."

Costas took the points and put them to the opposition.

Hard-eyes dismissed them with a shrug and a few sharp words which were pungently translated. What did they expect of a house in a historic village where the houses were all old. It was their very age that gave them their character and charm. Admittedly this old house might need a little renovation here and there perhaps, and in other ways improved if they wished to 'modernise' it. But that was up to them when it was theirs.

"It's not yet *when*," said John "it's *if*."

"If what?" the patient Costas asked.

"If the price is right."

When this was explained to Hard-eyes, he permitted himself a small indulgent smile as he gave Costas his reply. At the ridiculously low price his wife was prepared to accept for it, the house was a gift from heaven.

"How much?"

Costas hesitated, then encouraged by a nod from Hard-eyes mentioned an outrageous sum.

"That's not just ridiculous," said John "it's totally absurd."

More cold beer was ordered to cool the flaming argument which followed. Dimitri ambled to and fro with frosty bottles which only fired instead of cooled it. An hour went by in heated disputation. John made an offer, then in response to a nudge from Vivian, reduced it. Hard-eyes promptly raised his price. Costas in the middle, rolled his eyes from side to side, and occasionally heaven-wards as he interpreted the uninhibited exchanges.

"The property is unique..."

"Certainly the house is. The woodworms must be holding hands to keep the ceiling beams from falling..."

The afternoon, the argument and the beer steadily grew hotter. Hard-eyes held his ground. John and Vivian with gestures of despair haggled, frowned and bullied, cajoled and coaxed with the promise of hard cash. All to no avail. After a couple of hours they got up to leave. The other two with startled glances exchanged a few swift words in Greek.

"Sit down," said Costas. "I think we can come to an agreement." They settled for £200.

The next day the owner smiled bravely through her tears as she counted and pocketed the money, but her husband forgot himself so far as to grin contentedly as he handed over the deeds, knowing well that after another winter the house would be unsaleable.

In the short time left to them, John, Vivian and Deirdre camped in the house by day and began to plan. They measured, sketched and photographed and wrote innumerable notes, so that they could decide upon the necessary repairs and additions to be put in hand when they returned, whenever that might be.

Deirdre, the only one of the three still enchanted by the house, rushed about excitedly with a measuring tape and stood proudly in the foreground of every snapshot.

One afternoon as they were standing in the garden, a village woman came along the path carrying a pail of water. She was small and rather stout, and as she passed she nodded with a smile, then walked down to the donkey stable which was already being improvised into a kitchen of sorts for lunches, as the byre still had its uses. After a little while, curious to discover what she might be doing, they followed and found her washing up their lunch plates.

In the villages of Cyprus in those days, newcomers were looked after by their neighbours, a charming and friendly custom. This was how they first met their next-door neighbour Vassilia, who was to be their house-help for many years. Andreas her husband appeared the next day. He was a mason who later was to help in the rebuilding of the house and in many other ways. Both were warm and cheerful and eager to welcome their new neighbours who took to them at once. The house was hardly 'a gift from heaven' but Vassilia and Andreas were. They were to become close and stalwart friends to be blessed each passing day and year.

The house, roughly boarded up, the front door secured and the roof cracks sealed, was left in their charge till John and Vivian were able to return. Both John and Vivian were doctors working in Arabia[1]. In a few years time, having served there for fifteen years, their medical aspirations would have been fulfilled, and John at the age of fifty would be eligible for a pension. They would then retire from medicine to devote themselves to deep ambitions for which they had long prepared. Vivian to the fulltime pursuit of painting in which she had already proved her talent, and John to the composition of many songs he felt within him. They had often discussed the risks of abandoning a sure livelihood so early in their lives, but always agreed that they must accept them before it was too late to realise their hopes.

"After a year or two we might find ourselves running out of ideas or our abilities," John had sometimes said. "What would we do then? We might be too rusty and out of practice to return to medicine."

---

[1] Kuwait

"We have to trust in our convictions," Vivian would reply. "One road is ending and another which we've always hoped for, opens. We must take it and explore it. If we don't we'll never forgive ourselves for missing the moment of truth."

They had agreed that what mattered most before you died, was to discover what above all else you felt the need to do, and then to do it. It was no use complaining just before the coffin nails were hammered in, "I wish I'd had the chance to do what I always wanted to." Both were sure in their convictions and eager to put them to the test. But until that longed-for day they would have to continue in Arabia and prepare for it from there.

The first thing to be done was to plan the house, and the first decision to be made was what to do with the existing ruin. Should or could it be restored and embodied in the new extensions? Or should it be destroyed?
"Let's keep what can be saved," said Vivian. "It does have some character as Hard-eyes claimed, and it matches the other village houses as an entirely new house wouldn't. And the view from the windows which seduced us should surely be preserved."
"Agreed," said John "We'll tear out all that's rotten, rebuild it and extend into the garden with our additions." That crucial decision agreed upon, they were ready to start planning the extensions.

In the evenings, after busy days they sat down to exchange their thoughts and tentative suggestions. Problems which seemed simple enough at first, gave rise to discussion and lengthy argument. Sketches were drawn, defended by one, attacked by the other, then scrapped. More and more were produced, debated and rejected. But slowly, after many months as their ideas grew and came together, the plan progressed till at last it satisfied them both.

Downstairs, the donkey stable was to be converted to a kitchen-dining room, and the fodder store to a bathroom-lavatory. A stair would connect the floors. Upstairs, the living room was to be extended into the garden, the new united with the old by a wide embracing arch of local stone in the traditional manner. The decrepit bedroom would become John's study, and a new and larger bedroom would be added alongside the addition to the living-room. Every room would have its view of garden, hill or sea. The whole house would be spanned by a pitched tiled roof to thrust off summer heat and winter rains. From the outside the house would not conflict with the pattern of other village houses, having grown as a natural extension to the old. Inside, ceilings of woven reeds supported by slender beams, tiled floors, and louvered window shutters would retain its village character.

The house would be simple, compact and convenient, cool in summer, snug and secure from rain and storm in winter. Now the plan must be presented to an architect who might accept it and undertake the building. So Vivian went off to Cyprus taking Deirdre with her on a long school holiday. By great good luck she found an excellent architect at once, but like all good architects he had his own ideas and was less than hesitant in expounding them. The plan, he said, was simple enough of course as all plans dreamt up by amateurs inevitably were. Practicalities tended to be forgotten, subtle opportunities were missed. He smiled patiently as he neatly sketched alternatives here and there which though obvious to him were not immediately to Vivian. Amiable discussion soon cooled to polite but stubborn disputation. Disagreements about the rebuilding of a house were no less obstinate it seemed, than the buying of it had been. After much persuasion Vivian accepted some detailed changes to the plan which certainly improved it though the original conception remained intact.

Honour thus satisfied on both sides, drawings were produced, a contract was signed, masons, carpenters and plumbers were engaged and work began. The old ruin was soon reduced to its skeleton of a few bare walls. In front of it the garden was cleared and levelled while mules and donkeys plodded up the hill with bricks and mortar, stone and wood, pipes and tiles, then down again laden with chunks of concrete from the old roof, rubble from unsound walls and lighter loads of rotten beams and window frames.

Each morning Vivian came from the nearby house where she and Deirdre were staying, to discuss progress with the master mason Charalambos, a sprightly, straight-backed old man, wise and shrewd and a master of many skills. He was as fastidious a carpenter as a mason, and insisted upon his own high standards whatever the cost might be. Vivian readily agreed with that. Her only anxiety was that all the workmen would be there and working every morning. When she had counted them and was satisfied that all was going well, she and Deirdre would go off to the hills with a picnic lunch, Vivian to paint and Deirdre to wander and explore with a goat-bell round her neck in case she strayed too far. Often Deirdre would stay behind to play with Vassilia's four small daughters, and being lively and gregarious she soon knew every family in the village - firm roots for later friendships. It was a happy and fruitful holiday, filled with exciting expectation as the house began to grow.

The building had steadily progressed while Vivian had been on the spot to urge it on, and when she returned some three months later from Arabia, she expected to find it well advanced. But to her dismay she found that all work had stopped. Everything was just as it had been when she left. Tools lay about, but not a workman was to be seen. After a lengthy search she managed to trap the contractor in his house. He was evidently surprised but not embarrassed. To Vivian's heated remonstrations he replied with smiles and shrugs and cheerful reassurances, chiefly consisting of the word *avrio* tomorrow. Next day the work did indeed begin again, but only till another *avrio* which was the day after Vivian had left again, as she subsequently discovered. This exasperating situation was eventually resolved by sudden unannounced visits at every opportunity, and needless to say, on each occasion by much impassioned argument.

On one such visit Vivian took with her a sketch plan for her studio which had been almost as warmly debated as the house plan had been.

"I want a great big studio with lots of light and space to store my pictures," Vivian had said.

"Well, we can only do what's possible. I think you'll have to settle for something a little smaller," said John who at that time was absorbed in the planning of a hospital, and had perhaps become infected by too close association with architects. Like them, his views tended to be emphatic.

"What you need," he said "is a room about the size of a two-bed ward, twelve by sixteen feet."

"But that's not nearly big enough. I don't need a ward. I'm alive and well and want a studio."

"Of course, but there's only one place for it, at the bottom of the garden which is already small enough. If the studio is going to be as big as you'd like it to be, there'll be no garden left between the studio and the house."

Vivian already had firm ideas about the garden. It must be allowed to grow wildly without encroachment, a little Douanier Rousseau jungle full of mysteries to be explored and painted. Nothing must disturb or threaten it. So she planned a tall studio at its farthest edge, with large windows to admit light and sight. Inside, tiers of shelves along the walls would hold her canvases, paints and brushes and her finished pictures, leaving plenty of floor space for her daily work. When she showed her plan to the architect, he accepted it with an understanding smile as he sat at his cluttered desk amidst the unplanned chaos of his own office.

At long last the house and the studio were finished. John and Vivian and Deirdre all went off together for the great occasion, which was enhanced by a happy coincidence. Their old house in Scotland had been sold and the furniture had arrived in the village exactly in time to be put into the new one.

But their last and chief concern was for the garden. Now that the building rubbish had been cleared away it was revealed again as a bare neglected patch. They stood with Charalambos, looking at the starved and stunted trees, a lemon, an orange and two mandarins, still just surviving among weeds in the hard, much-trampled earth. The trees must be revived and much else also planted if the small wilderness was to become once more a garden. What was to be done? They turned to Charalambos. The spry old master mason like all village Cypriots, was an expert gardener. He looked at the hard dry ground and scratched his crisp white hair.

"Dig up. Put in plenty soil," he said.

"Well, we've got the soil," said John.

"Very little. All clay and stones. Dig all out. Put in good soil. Then manure."

Andreas who had joined them nodded in agreement.

"I bring carob soil from the hill and goat manure," he said, "and take stones for my garden path."

"What about water?" Vivian asked.

The old man spread his arms. "In summer must have plenty. I build big water tank and channels to trees and plants."

"What else?" John asked with growing apprehension.

Charalambos pointed to the edge of the garden where it reached the top of the cliff. "In winter we have big rain, too much water then. You lose much garden there. Must have strong wall to keep it."

John and Vivian looked at the crumbling edge. It was easy enough to imagine that every year the winter rains must have eroded it inch by inch. They fetched the Land Registry map that had been given them with the deeds, and measured the width of the garden shown on the plot, against its present width. It had been reduced, not just by inches, but by fifteen feet. The cliff-top wall was obviously an urgent need, and scarcely less so, a plentiful supply of water to the trees and a newly planted garden. John and Vivian turned again to their wise old friend.

"How much will it cost to build the wall, the big tank and the water channels?"

"About three hundred pounds."

"That's more than we paid for the house."

"Old house. Old garden. You spend plenty money to make old house new. If you want new garden, you spend some more."

The building of the wall, the tanks and channels would take some months, and the renewal of the garden many more as Andreas dug out the clay and stones and replaced them with rich black soil from the hillside. With the weary task completed and the new earth by then well-watered, the trees were soon to show signs of recovery, putting out new leaves and blossoms. Vines, bougainvillea, convolvulus, leafy plants and flowering shrubs would be planted in profusion to take root and flourish, promising the little jungle that Vivian had set her heart upon.

But these as yet were still just distant hopes. The immediate preoccupation was the furnishing of the house. Mules and donkeys struggled up the hill again, loudly complaining under heavy loads. Among their lighter burdens were two treasured decorations for the garden, a plaster copy of the Apollo Belvedere head, to be mounted in the centre of a fish pond in the middle of the garden, and another, of the head of Michelangelo's 'Dying Slave' to be set into a whitewashed garden wall. Apollo the very symbol of imperious life would shine in blazing sunlight, The Dying Slave would dream in dappled shade as a reminder that the span of life is short even in the presence of the Sun-god.

While Vivian and John, encouraged by the ebullient Deirdre, were busy in the house unpacking beds and chairs and tables, Charalambos outside was finishing a sunken patio. One morning it occurred to Vivian that he was taking rather longer than expected, so she went down to have a look at it, and chat with him. To her surprise, in the middle of the patio he was constructing a huge round, tiled table. It looked just right but had not been planned.

"What's that for?" she asked.
"When all finished," said Charalambos with a wink, "we have big feast. Many people. Need big table."

In accord with village custom, he explained, the owners of a new house were expected to celebrate the occasion with all who had contributed to the building. It was a natural expectation to which John and Vivian happily responded. The timely prediction, "Many people. Need big table" in the event proved rather modest.

On the festive evening the table was laden with chicken kebabs, roasted lamb and kid, salads and local dishes and carafes of wine and brandy. Charalambos with his retinue of masons, carpenters and plumbers, some bringing their wives and children, Andreas and Vassilia and many other village friends, all came to join the feast and bless the house. The food was eaten down to bones and empty plates. Glasses and carafes were emptied and re-filled. Tongues when not otherwise engaged were loosened in toasts as generous as the appetites, "Ya hara" *be happy*, "E viva" *to life*. The moon rose above the hill. Under the pale light the village sprawled asleep, huddled about the mother abbey.

The sated guests had fallen into silence. "The house must have a name," someone murmured, "What are you going to call it?"
"Irini. *Peace.*" said Vivian.

Years later during the troubles that were to come, Vivian once remarked, "Perhaps we should have called it War and Peace!" But on that evening, such a thought was not even to be imagined.

Leaving the garden and the house in the sure care of Andreas and Vassilia, they returned once more to Arabia. In that far desert all their thoughts and dreams at the end of every busy day, turned to the village, the house, the growing garden and their aspirations. The abbey bell kept chiming in their minds, summoning insistently. One day it chimed for them, and they left the hurly-burly outer life of Medicine, to explore their inner lives.

THE BELL PEALS

Bellapais had never looked so beautiful it seemed to John and Vivian as they arrived on one May morning and walked up to the house which for the rest of their lives was to be their home. It had been opened and prepared by Andreas and Vassilia who welcomed them at the door. They rushed inside and stood for a moment at a window to gaze at the quiet village spread below them.

"Come on!" said Vivian tugging John away. "You ought to know that view by heart. Let's go and see the garden."

It had grown beyond all their expectations. The four old citrus trees were alive again and fruiting. Lilies, roses, geraniums and plumbago, bougainvillea and convolvulus were flourishing, and the vines in full leaf were showing their first small budding grapes. The air was scented with flowers, and the earth watered from the big tank an hour or two before, smelled fresh and sweet. All was secure within the long white fortress wall above the cliff-top. The house at one end of the garden and the studio at the other had been newly white-washed.

"It looks a little like an Ivory Tower," said Vivian.

"Just right," said John.

The first few weeks were spent in thoughtless bliss, soon however to be disturbed by the arrival of their luggage. After fifteen years in Arabia there was not a little. Mules and donkeys laboured up the hill again. Their braying protests needed no translation, "Aaargh-hic-Aaargh" was plainly "Enough is enough!" But with much persuasion they brought all safely up.

The unpacking and disposal of the luggage took them many weeks, during which they were further engaged with the problems and perplexities of a simple village life which at first was simple only in its unsophistication. Drinking water was to be fetched each day in chatties from a hillside spring. Meals were cooked on a smoky paraffin stove. Since there was no electricity, the house was lit in the evenings by Aladdin lamps which proved less magical than the name suggested. Simple provisions were to be found in the two small village shops, though scarcely enough to subsist upon. Ice, much needed in the sweltering summer months, had to be brought from Kyrenia four miles away. A large block would be strapped to a front mudguard of a village bus, the only place for it as every inch inside was always crammed with villagers. As the bus crawled, radiator boiling up the hill, all eyes would be riveted to the precious cargo dripping irretrievably away beneath the scorching sun. The only trace that usually remained of it was a wet but quickly drying mudguard.

After a year or two, things were slowly to improve. Drinking water came to the taps. Dirty paraffin was to be replaced by clean Calor gas, the kitchen walls stayed white and food tasted better. Some years later electricity was brought to the village, thus ending the evening struggles with flaming paraffin lamps. Time wasted in daily shopping for fresh food, was saved by a refrigerator which also produced quantities of solid ice. Later still water heaters and washing machines were installed. All these conveniences were eventually to bring release from household chores to long mornings battling with the real problems of painting and composition.

But no such expectations occurred to John and Vivian as they busily unpacked and stowed away their luggage, and gradually acquainted themselves with the realities of the new life they had chosen. To be at last in Bellapais was happiness enough.

The house was full, except for one empty space in the living room awaiting a Steinway grand piano to be shipped from London. John had bought it on an irresistible impulse without a thought of the difficulties of its final transportation. It arrived one day at the port of Famagusta some fifty miles away. How was it to be brought safely to Bellapais and then up to the house? The more John thought about it the more impossible it seemed. Solomos, one of the village bus drivers came to the rescue. A cheerful and resourceful man, no problem however unfamiliar seemed to daunt him. As he stood at the door one evening expounding his proposal, his craggy features were split by a confident grin between an enormous nose and a formidable chin.

"I bring piano with my bus," he said.

"With your bus!"

"Sure."

"You'd never get it in. It's far too big."

"I put it on the roof."

"But it'd fall off coming up the hill, and anyway there'd be no room for it. The roof of your bus is always jam-packed with bicycles, crates of chickens, sacks of flour, barrels of wine, maybe a goat or two and god knows what else."

Solomos grinned patiently. "Won't fall off. I tie it good and strong. And plenty room. I make special trip with empty bus."

"But how would you get it off again? There's no crane in the village."

"I get it off OK."

"Well what then? You can get your bus as far as the bottom of the hill below the house, but how are you going to get the damn thing up the hill path? It's very, very heavy."

"Don't worry. I got it all worked out."

So next day early in the morning, Solomos drove to Famagusta, John and Vivian following in their car. When they arrived at the dockside warehouse and saw the gigantic packing case with its precious contents, their hearts sank and almost stopped as it was hoisted, dangling precariously at the end of a thin crane cable onto the top of the bus. Their spirits rose a little as they watched Solomos working like a spider to secure his catch in a web of ropes and straps. When he was satisfied that it was safe, he jumped down, climbed aboard and with a cheerful parting wave and no ears for John's "Drive slowly" sped away.

John and Vivian caught up with him on the long steep hill leading to the village. Solomos was grinding the gears. With ominous halts and lurches the bus crept up the hill. Would the sharply tilting packing case suddenly burst its ties and crash to ruination on the road, a jangling wreck of tangled strings and shattered dreams? It didn't. The bus groaned to the summit, slipped through the winding village streets and came neatly to a stop at the foot of the hill path beneath the house. Solomos jumped down still grinning.
"OK?" he said.
"Very OK so far. But how the hell are you going to get it up the path?"
"I got twenty men. Young men. Very strong. They carry it."
"With God's help perhaps. It weighs more than half a ton."

The young men came, bringing two long iron water pipes which were put down on the path, level with the cunningly positioned bus top. Then swarming round the packing case, they tugged and pushed and eased it squarely onto the pipes. Five men took each of the pipe-ends projecting in front and behind, lifted, and carrying their load like a litter they staggered up the narrow rocky hill path. It took them about two hours with many rests to reach the gate. Impasse! The packing case, even turned onto its narrow side would not go through.

The exhausted men were plied with beer to revive them for the next move, whatever that might be. While they stood about, nursing blistered hands and aching arms, Solomos was measuring the width of the gate against the thickness of the packing case. His grin had faded, but only for a moment.

"Unpack here." he said. "Plenty room with no packing case, six inches, if piano turned on side."

"But on its narrow side it can't be carried on the pipes. It'd topple over. And there's no room for the men to squeeze through carrying with their hands. Even if there was it'd have to be pushed and pulled along the cobbled path and that'd scrape the side off."

While Solomos considered this, Vivian suggested the solution.

"We have two old mattresses in the house. Why not put them underneath the thing and drag it to the house?"

"Bravo!" said Solomos, his fading grin returning.

The case was quickly stripped away, later to be claimed by Andreas for a chicken house. The naked piano was now a very awkwardly shaped load. There was hardly room for twenty pairs of hands to find firm grips. It must be lifted from its flat position, turned in mid-air then lowered on its narrow side upon the mattresses. The possibility of disaster was all too obvious. But the men refreshed and cheerful were undaunted. Swigging the last of their beer and promised more, they took up their positions and awaited their instructions.

"I tell you when." said Solomos. "OK?"

Heads nodded.

"And for the love of God don't drop it," John said.

"Lift!" called Solomos.

Every muscle strained. The piano slowly rose.

"Turn!"

As the piano tilted to the vertical, some handholds had quickly to be shifted, leaving the strongest to bear the sudden extra weight. John closed his eyes and prayed.

"OK. Now put slowly down," said Solomos.

A few feet staggered but no hand slipped as the piano came to rest with a resounding thump upon the mattresses, and then was swiftly shoved and tugged along the path into the house where it was held, happily right side up while its own firm legs were slotted in.

There stood the great gleaming instrument at last, unscathed, and beside it Solomos triumphant with his twenty strong young heroes. They were very thirsty, and as they downed their beer and called for more, they said to John "Play something. Let's hear if the thing still works!"

John happily though somewhat anxiously obliged. How would the piano sound after all the hazards of its journey? To his delighted astonishment it was perfectly in tune. The C sharp suggesting a troubled minor key expressive of anxieties and doubts, exactly matched the D flat of a blander major key which the abbey bell was pealing, it seemed in welcome at that joyful moment.

With the arrival of the piano, John and Vivian settled down each morning to six hours of uninterrupted work, Vivian in her studio, John in his study or at the piano. The gate was closed. No visitors were welcome. Even if they visited each other they did so with hesitation, knocking gently on the door. Vivian would sometimes come across the garden bringing a half-finished picture to discuss for a minute with John.

"What do you think of it so far?" she would ask.

John glancing at it impatiently, would say perhaps, "Not bad, but you need a bit more red in the middle." or "Surely that rhythm should be repeated?" or "Just sign it. It's complete."

Then having done his duty, he might say, "While you're here, tell me what you think of this."

He would play a few bars, and turning again to Vivian would find her still gazing at her picture!

"Were you listening?"

"Um, yes. Don't much like it, too dissonant." or "It's fine, don't change a note of it." would come the answer.

They understood each other's strivings and intentions so well that they always spoke the truth however disagreeable it might be. Disagreements are stimulating, but doubts may be corrosive. Vivian, happy in her elements, had no doubts. John did. He struggled eagerly but to little purpose. "Why?" he asked himself. At first he blamed the troubles in the island which occasionally disturbed the peaceful village. There came a day when invasion by a Turkish fleet was rumoured. Men and women stood on their rooftops gazing out to sea. Neighbours oiled and tested locks and bolts on house doors. Women ran to the streets calling to their children. Young men appeared with cartridge belts and rifles.

The crisis passed but the mood remained, till one day the cause of it came suddenly to John. He was caught up with guilt at having abandoned a useful life to follow a selfish ambition. Guilt breeds doubt, and doubt corrodes self-confidence. The diagnosis was a revelation and fortunately there was a remedy. Since there was no doctor in the village, he could be at least of some use to the villagers. He and Vivian had often discussed the possibility of holding a daily 'consulting hour' in the house, and for many reasons had dismissed it as quite impracticable. But they could help whenever called upon for simple medical advice and in emergencies, a sudden pain, a fever or an injured limb perhaps. Conscience was somewhat pacified and slowly confidence returned. John wrote a song which at last he could believe in, and was never again to regret that fretful change from medicine to music.

During their visits from Arabia, John and Vivian had made some friends among the villagers, of whom there were about nine hundred, all Greek Cypriots. Now that they had become villagers themselves they made many more.

It was a close community since there was much intermarriage within the village. A few of the older women had hardly ever left it. Naturally the attitude towards intruders was somewhat reserved. Visitors to the abbey were readily enough accepted. They just came for an hour or so and left, and rather more than twenty years ago there were not many of them. But how would the two outsiders be received, having bought a house and come to stay, the first foreigners to do so? (Deirdre was away at school in England and would only occasionally join them). Their friends were warmly welcoming. Others, as was to be expected, were rather cool at first, but when they had decided that the strangers seemed to be quite harmless, they thawed and accepted them with their generous hospitality.

Soon John and Vivian were being welcomed at street doors and invited to come in or at least to stop and talk. Chairs would be produced, *glikes*, walnuts or orange peel preserved in sweet syrup would be brought while they were bombarded with eager questions. How many children did they have? (Always the first question). Where had they come from, and what was it like in their own country? How did they like Bellapais, was it not the most beautiful village in the world? (Some who asked that question had scarcely seen another).
John and Vivian, having as yet no Greek themselves, could only guess at the gist of these and many other questions and cheerfully respond with nods and smiles. But from such unpromising beginnings happy friendships were to grow.

The villagers lived simple frugal lives, worked hard and lived to great old age. The men worked mostly in the fields, tending small holdings of vegetables or wheat and olive and citrus trees. The lemon trees, perhaps the best in the island were valued most. A good tree would produce several thousands of fat juicy lemons every year, earning for its owner twenty pounds or more, so a fair-sized orchard provided a comfortable income. Oranges, grapefruit, mandarins and tangerines were also grown in quantity. Olive trees were owned by almost everyone, and it was not unusual for a large old tree to be part-owned by perhaps three people. They grew as naturally in dry soil as the hardy and ubiquitous figs, but the fruit, unless plumped by timely rains, were small and for the most part fit only to be pressed for oil, and the back-breaking labour of stooping to gather them from the ground after the trees had been shaken and beaten several times, taxed the patience and devotion of even the closest families, the traditional task expected of them. The carob, a native tree needing no cultivation and easily harvested, provided a useful crop for a variety of purposes. The long black bean pods when ripe were used for animal food, (they were 'the husks which the swine did eat'), for sweetening other foods, for toffee sold at village fairs, and at one time for stiffening gramophone records.

The older men worked in the orchards and the fields, riding out on donkeys in the mornings with spades over their shoulders, or long poles to beat the trees. A few of them were shepherds or goatherds, wandering far along the hillsides with their flocks. All wore the traditional peasant dress of black baggy knee-length breeches, stockings and shoes or tall boots, white shirts and black sleeveless jackets. The younger men dressed conventionally. They were tradesmen and shopkeepers, butchers, artisans, carpenters or masons, some working in the village, others further away in Kyrenia or Nicosia where they were taken early in the mornings by a village bus which collected and brought them home again each evening. Between the old and young there were the village elders, who presided, watched and taught, keeping the villagers alive to their peaceful heritage - the Muchtar, the priest, the headmaster of the school, and the custodian of the abbey.

The women were kept busy in their houses, except at harvest times when they helped their men in the fields, reaping wheat, and gathering olives, almonds and walnuts from the orchards. They were devoted mothers, cheerful and indefatigable housewives, forever cooking, baking bread, scrubbing and sweeping, sewing the household linen and clothes for their families. Outside in their small gardens there were other chores to be attended to, vegetable beds to be nursed and watered, hens and chickens, turkeys, perhaps a clutch of guinea fowl and a goat or two to be looked after, and also vines and fruit trees, among them always a lemon and usually a mulberry tree.

The mulberry leaves were essential food for the silkworms which they bred each year. When the fat cocoons were ready they were tossed into a cauldron of boiling water, a gruesome spectacle presided over by the women. The long golden threads were extracted as they floated on the surface, to be spun on ancient spindles, then later woven on hand-looms into the silken cloth from which the women cut and fashioned blouses, frocks and skirts for their daughters, and shirts for their sons and husbands. The mothers, though restricted to what they could raise in their gardens or buy in the village shops, managed to feed their families as adequately as they clothed them.

The daily fare was simple but sufficient. Newly-baked bread, eggs, salads, yoghurt, cheeses freshly made from goat or sheep milk, olives and all fruit in abundance. Meat was usually eaten only at weekends when roasts of chicken, lamb or kid would be produced, and occasionally in the hunting season the men would bring in a partridge or a hare from the hill. For the women and children there was goat milk, orange or lemon juice to drink, and for the men brandy and the rough red local wine. On feast days the tables would be heaped with sumptuous food which for days the women had been labouring to prepare. There would be loaves of steaming bread flavoured with sesame seeds or whole olives embedded in them, chickens or perhaps a turkey surrounded by dozens of local dishes - *mezzes* of *hummus*, chick-peas, wheat or barley and other vegetables cooked in olive oil, vine leaves and marrows stuffed with rice or mincemeat, small fried fish, smoked ham, kebabs, home-made sausages spiced with herbs, sweetcakes and pastries made with honey, and wine of course in plenty.

Such gargantuan feasts were rare. The families subsisted contentedly enough on their frugal daily meals and nobody went hungry.

The children, because much loved, were happy and carefree, the girls dark-eyed, pretty and graceful, the boys lively and boisterous. Each morning they trooped off to the village school, neatly dressed in their uniforms, satchels strapped to their backs. They evidently enjoyed their lessons and their play outside surrounded by green trees and hills. As they grew up and left school, the girls returned to their mothers, helping with the housework, and learning in their turn to sew and cook while they awaited the day when they too would be married. The boys who had once carried baskets up to Irini for sixpences, suddenly became young men. Some disappeared and went abroad to study for careers, others remained to follow their fathers and sustain the continuity of village life.

As in most small enclosed communities, there were many 'characters' in the village. They were not eccentrics, just sturdy individuals. Their hard and simple lives shaped by fixed habits and traditions had made them what they were, conservative and stubbornly independent. Frangos who lived nearby, was one of the sturdiest and most engaging, an old man with a white thatch, a noble brow and a genial, gappy smile. His familiar straight-backed figure mounted on a mule, a long pole over his shoulder, suggested a latter day Don Quixote as he led his captive family, meekly following in the mornings to beat the olive trees. Often in the evenings John would meet him stumping slowly up the hill path in his great knee-boots after a long day in the fields. They would stop and gravely salute each other. The invariable greeting from Frangos was "Kalispera Kyrie Johnny" *Good evening Mr Johnny*. The Kyrie was pretty heady stuff at first, bringing to mind the Kyrie of Bach's B minor Mass. The Johnny was more comfortable, Vivian's usual name for John which the villagers had soon learnt. (Vivian herself was known as *Kyria Kathri*.) After a groping conversation which neither understood but solemnly pretended to, the ritual would end with a vice-like handshake as they went their ways.

One day, apparently curious to see the new house, Frangos came to the door, making as his excuse an apology for his vicious house dog Mavros which frequently savaged John when passing by and several times had bitten him. He had brought the snarling animal with him, hoping it might become more friendly. "Feed him. Won't bite then," said Frangos cheerfully. John gave the brute a crust of bread, then fetched a dressing for his bleeding fingers.

The door having been firmly closed on Mavros, Frangos sat down and surveyed the living room with little interest. His thoughts were evidently elsewhere. Wine was produced and thirstily accepted. There was some desultory attempt at conversation, but little communication. After a long silence, Frangos made plain his expectations. He turned to Vivian and said, "Pou ine to fayito Kyria?" *Where is the food Mrs?*
"Thellis ligo karpousi?" *Would you like some watermelon?*
"Ney, kai psomi parakalo." *Yes, and some bread please.*
Vivian fetched a very large water melon and a loaf of bread, plates and knife and fork which she put down before him at a table. Frangos, nodding in approval, drew up his chair, produced his own pruning knife from a pocket, and proceeded methodically and unhurriedly to demolish both the melon and the loaf, pausing occasionally to smack his lips and hold out his glass to be refilled with wine. When he had finished he sat back happily, burped modestly and winked with a beaming smile. "Poly orea spede," *Very good house,* he announced as he departed with the grinning Mavros.

There was Big Bacchus, so named by John and Vivian for his deep devotion to the grape. He was large, rubicund, cheerful and immensely strong. His chest was as big as the barrel of wine he delivered to the house from time to time. The barrel would be brought up to the gate on donkey-back. Big Bacchus would then shoulder it as lightly as a water chattie, and carry it down to the kitchen, there to be tapped and tested as he refreshed himself and pronounced upon it. However indifferent the wine might be, his verdict never varied.

"Is good. All wine good," he would say as he drained his glass and filled it up again.

"Not all wine," John would sometimes say. "Go easy with this stuff, it's pretty strong."

"Me very strong. Drink plenty."

"How much is *plenty*?"

His answer was hardly to be believed, though his thirst was evident enough. But his great strength was unimpaired, his eyes were clear and his hand was steady as he raised each brimming glass, spilling not a drop. At last, reluctantly conceding that he had, if not sufficiently, at least somewhat refreshed himself, he would slap his barrel chest, and with a vulpine grin repeat his credo "Me very strong" as he strode away no doubt in search of further sustenance elsewhere. Instead of blood, his veins must have flowed with strong red wine. He was surely a direct descendant of the great god Bacchus.

There was the enormous 'Poumpa', so dubbed by the villagers since he seemed to have been 'pumped up' like the Michelin Man, in fact over-pumped. The Michelin Man's integument was pressure-proof, but Poumpa's had burst in several conspicuous places, bulging in large hernias. Despite these embarrassments his smile was as constant as Mr Michelin's, and his close cropped Roman head gave him a certain jovial dignity. By trade he was a mason, surprisingly energetic when at work, less surprisingly much in need of rest during the heat of summer afternoons. For this, as he relaxed in the shade by Dimitri's coffee shop, four strong chairs were necessary - one to sit upon, one on either side to support his sprawling arms, and another in front with its back towards him to rest his head on. A fifth chair stood beside him for the cup of coffee to revive him when he woke.

When not thus occupied, his chief interest seemed to be in visitors or newcomers to the village. He was a *philexanos*, a lover of strangers, to whom he was drawn by a laughing curiosity and a natural generosity no less remarkable than that with which he had been physically endowed. If Vivian admired a rare plant in a rusty tin outside his door, next day the breathless Poumpa would stumble up the hill and present it to her. He took delight in giving, and lending a hand whenever something heavy had to be carried to the house, always with great gusts of laughter. He was a man of abundance in every sense of the word. John and Vivian were devoted to him, and this unwittingly led one day to an incident embarrassing to John, though happily not to the magnanimous Poumpa.

Two easy chairs were needed for the house, to be made by the village carpenter. Measurements were discussed. Height and length were soon agreed upon.
"How wide do you want them?" asked the carpenter.
"Better make them wide enough for Poumpa, then they'll be wide enough for anyone," John said airily. It was an unfortunate misjudgement. A few weeks later the chairs were brought up to the house, four strong men to each, helped by the panting Poumpa who sat down to rest himself in one of them. It fitted perfectly, the arms snugly embracing his hips.
"Very comfortable." he beamed.
John and Vivian sat down side by side on the other chair. They too were very comfortable with room to spare between them. The chairs had to be re-made. "Just make them half the width." John murmured with his apologies to the carpenter and a rueful glance at Poumpa enjoying the brief comfort of probably the only chair ever to match his amplitude.

When the new chairs were delivered, Poumpa stood by with bated breath as John and Vivian sat down in them. Would they fit this time? They did. The big man clapped his hands and went off laughing happily.

There was Poumpa's mother, an old, old woman, wrinkled, bent and blind, who sat alone in a shady corner of the square for hours in the mornings, spinning wool from an ancient bobbin which she dangled up and down between her wide-spread knees, obliviously absorbed in her fumbling occupation and her inmost thoughts. Her impassive face, white against her long black dress, gave no sign of what her thoughts might be. But sometimes as she sighed and talked softly to herself, she seemed perhaps to be dreaming of her childhood in the village nearly a hundred years ago.

There was another familiar figure, not so very much younger than Poumpa's mother, who was often to be seen walking beside his old grey-nosed donkey on the road to Kyrenia four miles away. He was tall, lean and upright, and strode with the gait of a young man. No one would have guessed his age, unless they had looked closely at his hooded half-blind eyes, his knotted hands, his traditional baggy breeches long washed out from black to grey, and his ancient worn out boots. He was over eighty. Most days he took his donkey down to a little bay near Kyrenia, dug sand to fill the saddle paniers and then walked up the hill to deliver his load to builders in the village. Despite the steepness of the road, he always walked to spare his donkey, laden or unladen. He made not one, but usually three journeys on a working day, sometimes four, more than twenty or thirty miles on his feet. He hardly ever spoke, just nodded and smiled contentedly as he sat alone in the evenings over a cup of coffee in the square.

There was Mr Alexis, small, straight-backed, lean and alert, not yet old but in the youth of his old age which he wore lightly after a long career as an officer of Police that had taken him to London with other chosen officials, for the coronation of the Queen. That had been his proudest moment, but he was well content to retire to his village, his family and his orchards. He rose very early in the mornings to dig and tend his much treasured trees. By ten o'clock, his day's work of six hard hours already done, he was usually to be found in one of the coffee shops sitting alone and thoughtful with a well-earned glass of wine, perhaps brooding over the exhausting task of harvesting his olives. After the trees had been shaken and beaten, the fruit had to be searched for and picked up one by one from the ground where they lay half-hidden among the twigs and leaves that had also fallen. The gatherers had to stoop for many hours, day after weary day. Surely there must be a simpler method?

Sometimes at that season of the year, John would sit with him to propose a better solution.

"Why not spread sheets on the ground to catch the olives as they fall, then gather up the sheets and empty them into your baskets? No stooping all day long. And you'd lose no olives hidden on the ground."

"We'd still have to sort out the olives from the twigs and leaves, and that takes hours."

"But you could do that sitting down at home. Much easier and more comfortable."

Mr Alexis, unconvinced, would invariably shrug and shake his head. The old familiar well-tried way was best. He was not a stubborn man, just rooted in the traditions of the village. New ideas were suspect, and in the course of his own career, seeking reliable evidence in support of dubious propositions, he had become a wary sceptic. But his natural resilience in retirement, his dry humour in reminiscence, and his devotion to his trees, had mellowed him. His gravely thoughtful face would often crease in a contented smile as he sipped his wine and spoke about his trees, reflecting that under his stern and unrelenting charge, they all flourished and were never disobedient. So his training as a disciplinarian still had fruitful applications. A wise man and a cherished friend.

There was the village 'Commie', a small rotund and meditative mason whose naturally cheerful disposition was ever at odds with his thoughts about the current situation, local or general, though his views were no more than puzzlements tinged with the palest pink. However well he might be doing he would never admit that life was any better than 'so and so', meaning 'so-so'.

"How are you doing?" John would ask him.

"Metric," *medium*, was the invariable reply.

"Oh come on, you seem to be doing fine."

His brow would frown and his mouth would smile in puzzled contradiction.

"No, only metric."

There was Bashi, short and very fat. Many of the older villagers grew rather thicker round the middle because they ate so much bread, their staple daily food. This was cheerfully enough accepted, so naturally was it a part of their placid slow-paced lives. They just grew plump as the fruit did on their trees. But Bashi's obesity, like Poumpa's was inborn. He was almost spherical and the constant butt of every village wag. This and his bodily discomfort made him highly irritable. Especially on hot days, he looked like a small aggressive bull as he stamped across the square with short quick steps, seeking a patch of shade to cool his sweating body and his boiling temper. His irritability was not lessened by the burden of ten young children whom he somehow managed to support with his earnings as a bus driver. However, he had his moments of revenge. Very early in the mornings when he had squeezed himself into the driver's seat of his old and battered bus, he would summon his passengers with long loud blasts on the horn, till the last and sleepiest of his tormentors had come running at his command, climbed aboard and paid his shilling to be taken to Kyrenia. Anyone who was late would have to walk. No one was ever late.

During the rest of the day he offered his bus as a taxi, charging his usual shilling to take even a single passenger to the very door of a house or shop in Kyrenia, wait for an hour or so if necessary, and bring him back for another shilling. He once drove Vivian to the airport twenty miles away, for which he asked ten shillings and would accept no more despite Vivian's urgings. When he was his own master he became a different man. Free of taunts he was open-hearted, generous beyond belief, often smiled and sometimes even laughed.

In the evenings, all the morning passengers would be gathered from their work sites and brought back to the village. But Bashi shifting forward in his seat to keep his short legs in contact with the pedals, would then begin to frown again. Tomorrow would be just another day of torments to be endured.

Opposite Irini, across a little stream there lived a very old man and his wife. Their house was a tumbledown old ruin shared by the birds which flew in and out through the broken window shutters and nested among the rafters. Grass sprouted thickly on the cracked and crumbling roof through which rain poured in the winters. There were two small mud-floored rooms, one furnished with a wide brass bedstead and a chair, the other with a paraffin stove, a cupboard, a rickety table and two kitchen chairs. Below there was the usual stable inhabited by an old white donkey. Outside the door, a lemon and an orange tree stood on a little patch of grass and weeds and wild flowers.

The white haired, bent old man earned a few shillings now and then from the sale of jasmine which he grew in rusty tins. In the mornings he crept about the garden, watering the trees and the jasmine plants or gathering sticks for firewood. Sometimes he came through the gate to see what John and Vivian were doing, standing and smiling with gentle curiosity, or inspecting a climbing jasmine they had bought from him. Once or twice a week he would venture a little further and return from a village shop with a couple of loaves clutched closely to his side. His ailing wife seemed to spend her days pottering about the house, sweeping, preparing an occasional meal or perhaps just resting on the great brass bedstead. But when it rained she would appear quite briskly to empty bucketfuls of water from the leaking roof into the stream, waving cheerfully to Vivian standing at a window of her studio and waving back.

On summer evenings the old couple sat outside their door, murmuring together as they gazed at the little unkempt garden. They sat serenely, like a lord and lady surveying their domain. Sometimes in the night John and Vivian would be called to give what help they could to the old woman, who perhaps had fallen or collapsed from weariness. The old man would come to the door, and peering with an anxious smile would say "Ella parakalo" *Please come*. Then taking Vivian's hand in one of his, he would light the way with a candle in the other.

The bare bedroom would be filled with worried relatives. What could be done? As John and Vivian stood by the bed, questioning, examining and holding a passive work-worn hand, they knew that nothing could be prescribed but rest and sleep. There was no cure for extreme old age. The old man standing in the flickering candle light would cup his ear and nod his head, pretending to understand. A few days later the indomitable old woman would be up and about again. In the evenings the two would be sitting outside once more, gazing silently and contentedly it seemed, at the familiar view of trees and flowers and the distant sea in the fading light, patiently waiting for their deaths.

A few paces from Irini, Andreas and Vassilia and their four young daughters, lived in a rambling house which had been mostly built by Andreas, room by room as the family increased. They were a closely devoted family. The girls all happily helped in the house, worked hard at their lessons in the village school, and at the end of the day would sit sewing the cloth their mother had woven on her loom, making dresses for themselves. Often Deirdre on holiday from Arabia, would join them as they stitched and giggled and sang songs to the rhythm of their needles. At an early age they were already preparing themselves for their destinies in marriage.

Vassilia, born to motherhood it seemed, gave all her watchful care to them, with never a thought for herself. Her instinct was so strong that even John and Vivian were embraced within it. Vivian though the same age as Vassilia, became Vassilia's *khori mou* (my daughter). And often after a morning's work in Irini she would come back from her own house with a plate of steaming food she had prepared for her family, to be shared.

Andreas, having fathered four daughters was faced with the alarming prospect of providing each of them when they married, with a house and furniture as their dowry, and also a wedding feast. All four daughters were duly married, at what cost to Andreas can only be imagined. It would surely have daunted a wealthy man. At the wedding of his last and youngest daughter, five hundred guests sat down at trestle tables in the garden of the house he had built with his own hands for her. Nothing was stinted. The tables were laden with as much food and wine as they could hold. And instead of one old fiddler, a four-piece band was hired for the dancing after the feast. Andreas was assuredly a man of character, self-reliant and responsible. He was also a most endearing 'character' in that other sense of the word. Despite his burdens he never seemed to have a worry in his head. There was an air of jauntiness about him. His hat was always tilted at a rakish angle above his Phoenician nose. His step was light and carefree, and he was always laughing. He was a hard bargainer as God knows he had to be, but having reached a reasonable agreement after much teasing argument, he would go off to build a wall or pave a path that would last for twenty years.

His friendship was as solid as his work. Often in the shooting season he would bring a brace of partridges or a hare and perhaps a woodcock. Once when 'troubles' had erupted in the island while John and Vivian were away, he sat for many nights unsleeping in Irini with a rifle beside him cocked and ready to protect it.

When all the girls were married, Vassilia became so preoccupied with grandchildren whom she mothered as devotedly as she had her daughters, that she had no time for house work in Irini.

In her place there appeared one day another redoubtable 'character' - Ulla Boola, ruddy complexioned, cheerful, very large and powerful. Such was her awesome strength that she would walk along the path to the house swinging a full gas cylinder in each hand as though they were mere baubles.

Her generosity, like Poumpa's, matched her size. Many mornings she would bring a loaf of bread just baked in her own oven, or half a dozen eggs still warm from the nest, or perhaps an armful of fresh vegetables from her garden. Her independence was no less remarkable than her generosity. Despite Vivian's suggestions, she went about her work just as she herself decided to, and with the energy of a hungry tigress. Upstairs, as furniture was upturned, whacked with dusters and put down again with thumps and squeaks, it sometimes sounded like a cat-fight. Downstairs in the kitchen, as pots, pans, plates and glasses were scrubbed and polished, (perhaps 'punished' would be a more appropriate word), the sounds were more orchestral, punctuated occasionally by a tinkling crash as a tumbler tumbled from her mighty hand. When she had finished her work inside the house, she would go outside to attack the garden, weeding, watering and sweeping paths. Not until she was satisfied that everything had been reduced to order would she consent to leave with a blessing and a beaming smile.

Within that driving force there was a surprising gentleness, the imprint of the village in which every individual grew as naturally as a tree. Ulla Boola, as sturdy as an olive tree though not perhaps as supple, was unmistakably her own unique and very self. She was dearly loved.

In the abbey square, there was the patient and benign Dimitri of the coffee shop who spent all day and half the night fetching coffee, drinks and snacks to 'freeloaders' and old men interminably swapping village chat, or just dozing and waking now and then to shout "Ella Dimitri!" *Come Dimitri*. In due time at his own unhurried pace, Dimitri would respond, bringing without further bidding, coffee, wine, brandy or beer to the villager who had called, knowing by his voice what his usual need would be. The pocket of his short apron seldom held more than a few small coins in return for his unceasing service. Nor did he seem to care. He was never heard to ask for payment. His only question, quietly murmured as he ambled sleepy-eyed from table to table was "Ti thellis?" *What would you like?* It seemed that long ago he had resigned himself to the role of village host.

The chief provisioner of the village was Anthimos, short and sturdy, cheerful and ever hopeful as he pressed his customers to buy his wares. The shelves of his small shop, a few steps from the square, were crammed to the ceiling with groceries of every kind, edible, drinkable, canned or bottled. The floor was littered with cases of fruit and vegetables, jars of olives, sacks of rice, lentils and dried beans, and sometimes a box or two of salted fish. On a large high table at the centre, bowls of eggs, stacks of loaves, and occasionally some cuts of newly slaughtered lamb, surrounded the altar of the weighing scales. In one corner there was a barrel of wine, and in another, safely distanced from it, a drum of paraffin so that even the thirstiest old man coming to refill his wine-stained gourd, could make no mistake.

Anthimos, presiding over his small emporium with an eager eye, missed nothing. At one moment he would be sitting at his desk, frowning as he scribbled orders to be paid for later. At another he would be on his feet persuading the less reluctant to pay in cash, or having spied a sly customer throwing in a couple of cucumbers to overweigh the scale, would toss them out again with a knowing smile.

In the afternoons when trade was slack, he would stand at the door with a wide-eyed and expectant "Yes?" to any passers-by, hoping to lure them inside. He was a hard-working, ebullient young man with an engaging sense of humour which he enjoyed no less than his devoted customers. Often in the evenings, John would look in to see what he had to offer. Over a glass of wine they would exchange an absurd patois of execrable Greek and English. It was a fine point as to whether Anthimos's English or John's Greek was the more atrocious, though they usually managed to understand each other.

"Echis any, er, neos, um, er, vegetables?" which was meant to mean, "Have you any fresh vegetables?" John asked on one occasion.

"Yes, plenty rubbish and garbage" Anthimos replied.

John was so familiar with their extraordinary jargon, that it took him but a moment to translate 'rubbish and garbage' into 'radish and cabbage'.

There was another villager, the ineffable George, whose English was even more resourceful and picturesque than Anthimos's. Never at a loss, he would fill the many gaps in his small vocabulary simply by using words that sounded roughly the same as those which eluded him. Thus, 'Lights' became 'Lice'. The parrots which he kept in cages, were 'Paris in their cases.' 'Cases' and 'cages' were a source of some confusion. "You like to buy a cage of wine?" Once, offering Vivian some carnation cuttings from his garden, he asked if she would like some 'coronation stinks', meaning of course 'carnation sticks' John and Vivian soon became expert in translating this enchanting language, practicing it together so that though they might not meet George for several months they were always well prepared.

On one such occasion John had put on weight and George had lost some. George looked at John, then at himself and said, "Think me. You very strong", which to the initiated could only mean, "I'm thin. You're very fat." The intrusive 'k' tacked onto 'thin' was admittedly a little puzzling for a moment, but only for a moment.

Lacking such imaginative inventiveness, John and Vivian decided that the Greek grammar books and dictionaries they had been struggling with were clearly not enough. They must learn to speak the language in simple conversation. So they took lessons in the evenings from a young village friend who was eager to learn spoken English in exchange. It was not a great success. The young man learned a smattering of pidgin English, and John and Vivian a few hard-won words and phrases of the demotic, usually mispronouncing them and forever stumbling over the frequent irregular verbs. How they wished that instead of Latin, they had been taught Greek at school. Some of their fellow-villagers evidently also did.

"Isighia," said John one evening, raising his glass to his old friend Nicos the Forester and one or two others sitting at a table in the square. Nicos put his glass down with a thump. "What's the matter?" John asked in some bewilderment. "I said *Isighia*, the old toast meaning *Peace*."

"We all know what you're trying to say," said Nicos patiently, "you're always saying it, but I think it's time we put you right. The word for peace is *isiyia* not *isighia*."

"Well what's the difference?"

"*Isighia* means *Shut up!*"

Nicos the district Forester, and the doting father of a family of eight, was big, benevolent and cheerful. His alert dark eyes always seemed to be waiting to be lit with laughter. He was a friend for all seasons and for all occasions. Under his wise advice and care, the little garden, the trees and vines, survived and flourished even during summer droughts and winter floods. He was a bon viveur, and all occasions were enlarged by his appetite for enjoyment and the sharing of it.

The happiest occasions were nights spent with him in one of the forest stations he was posted to from time to time. After a long day driving in the mountains, John and Vivian would arrive, sometimes with visiting friends, to find Nicos beside a smouldering charcoal fire threading thick slices of juicy meat onto spits to be slowly turned above the white hot embers. When Nicos judged them to be exactly ready, they were taken sizzling to be devoured with salads and good wine on his high balcony overlooking the tree-clad hills below. As the sun, the food and wine went down, Nicos would speak about his work, terracing the hills to catch rain water and conserve the soil, culling and planting trees, and persuading the local goatherds to feed their flocks, not in the forests but on the grassy plains below.

"I'm a very lucky man," he once said. "I love my work here in the mountains, and have many friends. My only enemies are soil erosion and the goats which strip my trees."

All his many friends would have agreed with that, counting themselves as also very lucky in his friendship. He was a much loved figure, a benign and jovial influence in the village.

But the man who dominated and ruled the village with an assured and easy power was the Muchtar, a man of force and unquestionable authority, held in respectful awe by the villagers and all who knew him. He had succeeded his father as Muchtar at the age of twenty seven, and was to remain in charge until his death some forty years later. His rule was absolute. The peaceful well-ordered life of the village reflected his unrelenting watchful care of everything that went on within it.

When John and Vivian first met him he was in early middle age. Their immediate impression was of solid physical strength. His massive shoulders and heavy build were evidence enough. His darkly brooding eyes and deep, husky voice gave warning of further formidable strengths which proclaimed him a man of conviction and decision. Later as they came to know him well, they gradually discovered the warmth and laughter and humanity beneath that stern appearance.

As a young man, adventurous and sometimes reckless by his own account, he had had his fling. But when he had succeeded his father as Muchtar he had settled down to his responsibilities as paterfamilias to the villagers, and put away his wilder impulses - all except one which still drew him irresistibly on occasion. He loved a gamble. On New Year's Eve he would sit in Dimitri's crowded coffee shop at a tric-trac board over the most exciting wager of the year. As the clock struck midnight, whoever had won most games would have the best fortune in the coming year. Or so it was believed. He always seemed to win, and perhaps there was something in the superstition, for he also always prospered.

He lived in an old house built of stones from the ruins of the abbey of which it seemed to be a part, standing in the abbey garden close beside the cloister. From his balcony he could look down upon his orchards, citrus, olives and almonds spreading into the distance, and call instructions to his gardeners. The property inherited from his father was meticulously cared for with deep pride and pleasure. The orchards flourished in abundance, and the house close to his possessions, to the abbey and the square, was perfectly positioned for the Muchtar at the centre of his domain.

Sometimes in the evenings, meeting by chance in the square, the Muchtar would take John and Vivian to the house to sit and talk over liberally poured drinks, and delicious local dishes produced by his dear wife Christala, gently smiling and warmly welcoming, who would never let them leave without a basketful of oranges, grapes or almonds from the orchards. The Muchtar, relaxed and eloquent, would speak about his many and various problems which called for much understanding of the villagers and occasionally for timely action. Remembering his own impulsive youth he kept a watchful eye upon the young, enjoying their natural exuberance but severely disapproving of any serious misbehaviour. One day the future of the village would be in their hands. He had learned his lessons. So must they.

Two stories illustrate the Muchtar in his maturity. The first he related himself as John and Vivian sat with him on his balcony.

A goatherd had complained to him that he had been losing goats while they were grazing on the hill above the village.

"Who's taking them?" the Muchtar asked.

"Boys from your village."

Next afternoon the Muchtar took his gun and went up the hill in search of partridges - and other quarry. As he was coming home he spotted a pale object hanging from a tree, half hidden beneath the branches. He quickened his step and came upon two village boys skinning a goat. Covering them with his gun, he sat down beside them on a rock.

"Where did you get that goat?" he growled.

"Up there," said one of the quivering boys.

"You stole and killed it?"

"Er, yes."

"Well in some countries you might be lynched for that. A nasty way to die. I'm just going to shoot you, then bury you with your goat. Nobody will know what happened to you."

He lectured them for half an hour and let them sweat as they pleaded for their lives.

"All right," he said. "I won't shoot you. I'll just hand you over to the police and make sure that you're jailed."

As he looked at the trembling boys he decided that they had had punishment enough. He put away his gun, and said quietly, "If you give me your word that you'll never do this again, I'll let you go and say nothing more about it. You'll pay the goatherd of course for this goat and for all the others you've stolen from him."

"We promise," said the boys.

At this point in his story, the Muchtar smiled and winked.

"Of course I wasn't going to shoot them or turn them over to the police. No use sending boys to jail, it just makes them worse. And anyway at their age I might have done the same as they did! They're both grown up and married now with sons who are very well behaved. We're good friends and often laugh about that day."

The other story which circulated round the village during one of the 'troubles' which beset the island, revealed the Muchtar at his most implacable when his authority on his own territory was challenged by anyone bold or foolish enough to do so. A military officer appeared in the square one day when the Muchtar was away and gave some orders to the villagers. When the Muchtar heard about it later he said "This is my village and I give all the orders in it." If that man came again he'd shoot him. The man did come again but evidently got the message, and believed it. He was seen hastily retreating, glancing fearfully over his shoulder, and never returned to face the Muchtar's wrath.

Each evening the Muchtar sat at a table in the square awaiting the villagers who would come to him with their problems. Knowing them all intimately, he could tell by the way they approached what their questions or complaints would be. As each man came across to him, the Muchtar would offer a chair, call for coffee, listen attentively then give his quick decision or advice. Sometimes it would be the Muchtar himself who did the questioning. A man might be summoned and challenged for some misdemeanour or sharp practice and severely reprimanded. The Muchtar, formidable in the extreme on such occasions, would sit crouched like a stalking lion, his eyes blazing, and in place of a lion's tail whisking before the leap, whirling a string of worry-beads dangling from one hand. He seldom had to roar. His basso profundo voice was frightening enough. The victim of his disapproval would not offend again.

Such incidents were rare. Usually the Muchtar would sit relaxed and thoughtful as he listened to a villager in need of his support or help. If the case was sound or at least deserving, the stern judge would become the ready advocate, and needless to say the problem would be resolved. The power of the judge-advocate was rooted in his intuitive sense of 'justness' and his decisiveness. In both he was immovable. For him the world was populated by 'good men' and 'rascals'. A good man must be supported. A friend remained a friend. A rascal could expect his due deserts.

On Sunday mornings, the Muchtar presided in the coffee shop at sales of land and property, collection of dues and other village business. After one such session he came up to Irini with news for John and Vivian. Their neighbour, an old woman who had been ailing for some months in hospital, had died. She had lived in a derelict house set on a small plot of stony ground immediately outside their front gate. Through her ground they had long ago bought a right of way from her since it was the only access to Irini.

"The old lady left her property to her elder son," said the Muchtar, "but he lives in another village and doesn't want it, so it's to be put up for sale by auction."

"What about her younger son?" Vivian asked. "He's unsettled and would surely be glad to have it?"

"He doesn't want it either. He's a wanderer, and rather witless as you know."

John and Vivian were well aware of that. He had sometimes come to spend a few weeks with his mother, and on one visit had left an embarrassing token of his witlessness. There was no latrine inside the house, and none outside. The usual arrangement in the village was an outside pit latrine, discreetly hidden in the garden among trees and bushes. Such an essential amenity was an obvious necessity even to the simplest-minded, so the younger son had decided to provide it. The grass and weeds growing in the bare stony plot gave no promise of modestly protective cover. But undeterred, he had dug a shallow pit, choosing to place it directly beside the gate, and surmounted by a kitchen chair in the seat of which a hole had been thoughtfully cut out. Occupied or unoccupied, and exposed to the general view it was not an ideal decoration to the entrance of Irini even for the least expectant visitors. John and Vivian had protested, as had the Muchtar on their behalf, but to no avail. Since the ground beyond the gate had belonged to the old lady she was free to use it as she chose, even to the indulgence of her simple-minded son.

"Well let's hope that the new owner will agree to remove that unsightly inconvenience," said John "We'll gladly pay him compensation."

"You won't have to," said the Muchtar. "You are going to be the owners."

"But we have our house and our small garden, and Vivian has her studio. We need nothing more."

"Listen," said the Muchtar with a weary smile "the property is right next to yours. You must buy it."

"Why?"

"Because if you don't some rascals will. And they might do worse things than putting a latrine outside your gate. They could cut off your access, fill the house with goats and chickens and make such a nuisance of themselves that you'd have to pay a ransom to get rid of them."

"I can't believe that anyone would do that to us!"

"There are one or two who might."

"Well, we'll just have to trust our luck on that. What would we use it for?"

"I don't know, but your house is small and one day you'll need more room."

"When is it to be auctioned?"

"On the second Sunday in September."

It was late July. John and Vivian were going away for two months holiday and would not be back in time.

"We won't be here," said John "so that's that."

"Oh no it's not. I'll put off the auction till you come back," said the Muchtar with a ferocious grin, "and then I'll bully you again."

When John and Vivian came back from their holiday, they had almost forgotten about the matter. Not so the Muchtar. He came to the house one evening and returned to the attack.

"The auction is fixed for Sunday week." he announced. "I've put up the necessary notice in small print, behind the coffee shop door where it can be seen, though not too easily, and I've told nobody except you about the sale. You'll have to buy the house. What are you prepared to offer?"

"Oh, it's worth nothing as it is. One room above a rough old donkey stable, and the roof and the upper floor both fallen in. It's just a heap of rubble, and outside is all weeds and stones We'd have to spend a small fortune to rebuild the house and plant a garden."

The Muchtar was in no mood for discussion or excuses. He had decided that the small property should naturally belong to John and Vivian and his decisions were inflexible.

"How much will you offer?" he persisted. "Tell me what you can afford and I'll get it for you."

"But if it's to be sold by auction, it'll have to go to the highest bidder, and that won't be me, though I don't expect there'll be much competition."

The Muchtar shrugged impatiently. "Let us see. Give me your offer," he growled.

Further resistance would be futile. John and Vivian were no match for the Muchtar in full force, and also it would be boorish to say the least, if they continued to oppose his concern on their behalf. John gave up the struggle. "Let's say sixty pounds," he said.

On the appointed Sunday morning John and Vivian went down to the coffee shop. At a table in the large bare room, the Muchtar sat with the son who had inherited the property. Around the walls sat about a dozen villagers, reading newspapers and pretending to take no interest. The Muchtar beckoned John and Vivian to join him and introduced them to the owner, a thin elderly man with a resigned but not uncheerful face, to whom the Muchtar turned and spoke in a rapid undertone.

"What were you saying to him?" John asked.

"He said he wanted £120, but I told him to expect £60."

The Muchtar then read out the description of the house, its position and the reason for its sale. Almost in the same breath he said "What am I bid?" and in a hoarse whisper to John, "Put in your bid."

"Sixty pounds," said John obediently.

One or two of the villagers had put down their papers and were looking thoughtful. The Muchtar glared at them, rapidly repeated his question "What am I bid?" the necessary three times, banged his fist on the table, rose to his feet and roared the one word "Sold!" He then turned to the bewildered and rather less than joyful John and Vivian "Now the property is yours, and no rascals can take it from you," he said with a triumphant smile. The whole procedure had taken perhaps five minutes. John produced the money, with which the owner seemed quite contented As he and the villagers departed, the Muchtar scribbling his official record of the sale, laughed and chuckled. "There were one or two rascals there who were thinking of out-bidding you," he said "but they were too slow making up their minds."

Now that it was theirs, John and Vivian began to take an interest in the little ruin. On the upper floor there was a fair-sized room which had been used for all purposes except the one provided by the gate. The donkey stable underneath was of an equal size. The roof and the upper floor would have to be restored, but the foundations and the walls were solid.

They decided to remake it into a little guest house, with a two bed sitting room upstairs, and a kitchen-eating room and a bathroom-lavatory downstairs. The stony plot would become a small patio paved with flagstones and shaded by an orange, a lemon tree and a vine beside a fish pond with a fountain in the middle. Andreas went to work on the reconstruction of the house, which took many months. Charalambos then returned to install the plumbing while Andreas shaped and paved the patio, planted the trees and the vine and built a circular pond to embrace the fountain at its centre. When all was finished, the house was painted white with yellow doors and window shutters to match the lemons and oranges when they appeared. The new patio soon became a favourite place on early summer mornings, to sit beside the pool where goldfish lay beneath the leaves of flowering water lilies, brightly coloured dragonflies hovered and circled the gently splashing fountain, and swallows flashing across the water, dipped to take small sips. It was a place for dreaming undisturbed, yet filled with the new life attracted by the pond.

The little house, transformed, attracted its own visitors.

Deirdre came home again from Spain where she had settled and become a Spanish dancer, bringing her husband (an American guitarist) and their small son. She also brought her castanets and Flamenco dresses, and dancing round the patio told of her adventures with the gypsy troupes she had joined to dance all over Spain. For ten exuberant years, old friends and many others newly found, came to stay for weekends and longer holidays, bringing news of the outer world and their own happiness to be shared. It had been a lively joyful chapter, but perforce it had to end. Vivian's studio had become so crammed with pictures that somewhere had to be found to store and show them. The guest house was the only place, and so it was to be. The Muchtar had said, "One day you'll need more room." How often Vivian and John blessed him for 'persuading' them to buy that small unlikely ruin.

Just as the days were measured by the natural village sounds, so were the seasons by their events. Spring came early, the first hint of it in mid-January when sometimes the first small buds appeared. By February the village was sprinkled pink and white with almond blossom, matched across the sea by the snow on the Taurus mountains, pink in the early morning sunshine, and later glistening white. Soon after, the returning swifts and swallows came shrieking in. The days were sometimes warm with clear skies. More often there were rain and thunder storms, or dry icy winds blowing from the snowclad Taurus.

Occasionally the village would wake to the quietness of snow which overnight had transformed the gardens and the hillside into an improbable Christmas landscape.

'March comes in like a lion and goes out like a lamb' - not always. The lion was often still raging till mid April, the most fickle month. But long before the end of March the lamb had appeared within its grazing flock, suckling, and nibbling the tender shoots of grass. March was the awakening month for the vines and trees, almonds, figs, walnuts, mulberries and the scarlet pomegranates, all coming into leaf. April was the month of wild flowers. Fields were carpeted with oxalis. Wayside paths were thickly bordered with mimosa, bright yellow daisies, tall fennel and the ghostly asphodel. The hills were speckled with cyclamen, ranuncula and the white iris planted in castle gardens by French crusaders, and now widely spread along the range. This was the time to go in the afternoons with trowels and baskets to search and dig for corms and bulbs and bring them home to be planted in the wild little garden where they soon took root among self-seeded narcissi, anemones, hyacinths, gentian, wild garlic and a host of unknown others snugly settled there beneath the figs and vines now appropriately in full promise of fruitfulness for the chief festival of the year.

Lent and Easter dominated village life during March and April. On the Sunday a week before Lent, small boys grotesquely masked, roamed the streets, knocked at doors and sang for sixpences. On the following Sunday (Carnival), the youths and adolescents had their day. Shrouded from head to foot in long white sheets, they appeared at doorsteps like unholy ghosts, to sing in ragged chorus. Then, absurdly disguising their voices, each in turn would grunt or squeak, "Guess who I am." When all guesses had proved wrong they revealed their familiar faces and ran laughing to the next house.

On the evening of Carnival Sunday, the villagers gathered in their houses for the last full meal before the Lenten fast which began the following day, "Green Monday", so-called because only green vegetables from their gardens would be allowed them for the next four weeks. No one fasted on that feasting night. In good time before the end of Lent, the women were busy in their kitchens preparing for the great feast of the year. Early on the morning of Good Friday, girls appeared in the streets carrying on their shoulders long bread-boards stacked with Easter loaves, baskets of Easter cakes and coloured eggs, to give to friends and neighbours. Towards midday the *Kopalles* (young women of marriageable age), dressed in bright new frocks, strolled in laughing groups around the square, followed by the keen glances of young men sporting their smartest suits.

On the eve of Easter Sunday, the old and young all gathered in the square again to watch a roaring bonfire. The young men now the centre of attraction, vied with each other to hurl ever huger logs onto the fire, glancing hopefully at the young woman for approving smiles, or to the older folk for their applause of shouts and cheers. The bonfire blazed and leapt in pagan celebration till the abbey bell began to peel for midnight mass. The strenuous antics ceased and the jubilant mood subsided as the performers and their audience, suddenly subdued to an obedient congregation, quietly assembled in the abbey where flickering candles lit the darkness with a light more luminous than the dying bonfire, and the voices of the cantors, rising in plainsong to the vault, filled the night air with benedictions.

As the congregation tumbled out from the church into the square, excited and elated at the dawn of Easter Day, the bell pealed as fast as it could be swung for an hour or longer, till the boys at the end of the rope could pull no more. Easter Day was given up to feasting. In every house, families with their relatives and guests sat down to roast chicken, lamb and other meats cooked in garden ovens. Tables were stacked with sesame bread and loaves with olives baked in them, innumerable local dishes, salads, hard-boiled coloured Easter eggs, spiced cakes, fruit, olives and almonds. Wine and brandy flowed again for the men till every thirst after four dry weeks had been appeased.

Easter was also the season for marriages, usually arranged by parents after dowries and other agreements had been settled. The wedding procession was a frequent sight as it wound through the streets from the abbey to the dowered house, the black-robed bearded priest in the lead, singing a blessing accompanied by a mandolinist or a fiddler, followed by the bride and groom both crowned with wreaths of orange blossom, and behind them a long bright trail of wedding guests. The nuptial feasts sometimes continued for two or three successive nights, parents and hosts of helpers roasting lamb and kid, mixing tubfuls of salads, tapping barrels of wine for the insatiable guests crowded at tables in small gardens. At some stage on the first night, the bridal mattress would be produced and to loud applause a chubby baby son would be rolled upon it by its mother, in ritual encouragement to the blushing newly-weds. After the guests had had their fill they danced to traditional tunes played by an old fiddler who scraped away as long as his glass was kept filled with wine, and his hourly fee was promptly paid.

The first of May was celebrated as the opening day of summer. Every street door was hung with a wreath of flowers. Vassilia came into the garden early in the morning to pick roses, lilies and geraniums, and sat deftly weaving them into a garland to be hung on the front door where it would remain and slowly wither for a year.

By June the water wardens were working all day long and often late into the night. One with a clock, the other with a spade, they went from house to house delivering irrigation water to the gardens. Precisely at a certain hour on his allotted day, each householder was given his due ration, strictly timed by the warden with the clock, while the other with his spade diverted the water from street aqueducts into garden channels for the house owner to distribute according to his needs - much for citrus trees, some for vegetables and flowers, but not a drop to be wasted on figs, olives or well grown vines which needed none. When 'Time' was called, the water was blocked off by a spadeful of earth and directed along the street to the next house.

At eleven o'clock on Thursday mornings, John and Vivian were ready in the garden with their spades to receive their share, most of it for the trees, the rest to fill the tank. In good years when the aquifers in the hills had been well filled with winter rains, the water came racing in such a torrent that sometimes it was not the time-keeper but themselves who shouted 'Stop'. Within twenty minutes the trees were drenched and the tank was full. After dry winters there was often scarcely enough to reach the farthest trees, and worse still, the time allowance would be cut short. Arguments naturally arose.

"We're due for seven more minutes."

"Not today."

"But we've paid for half an hour."

"Too littly (little) water."

"But the tank is empty. The plants will have no water for a week."

"Same for everybody. Very littly water."

The water wardens, always, and justly, won the arguments which sprang up at every garden gate. They had to share the water equally among everyone, whatever their 'entitlements'. In the evenings, their figures lit by lanterns, flickered along dark hill paths to distant gardens. Above the soft sounds of water the argument evidently continued, joined by the calling Skops owls mournfully measuring time with the persistence of a clock, and the scolding of the screech owls.

There were other and more tranquil occasions in the month of June. A choir, a string quartet, a small orchestra or a harpsichordist would come occasionally to give a concert in the abbey cloister by the light of a full moon augmented by great candles in tall brass candelabras from the abbey church. The pure sounds rising in the limpid air perfectly expressed the gentle spirit of the village, subdued beneath the abbey shining bone-white in the light. Long after the audience had departed, the air remained alive with the sound of nightingales singing in surrounding orchards.

July and August brought discomforts and distractions. Energies and spirits wilted. In unremitting heat it is not easy to concentrate or write a manuscript with sweat dripping onto the page, or to paint with cool detachment. Thoughts wander. Imagination sleeps. Ideas evaporate and refuse to grow. In vivid contrast, outside in the garden all life grew and flourished in profusion. Figs and pomegranates plumped and ripened. Grapes fattened in huge clusters. Lemons and oranges grew large on drooping boughs. All these of course were very welcome. But other forms of life that inevitably came with them, aroused a good deal less enthusiasm. Cicadas droned deafeningly and unceasingly from dawn to dusk. Great spiders spun their plate-sized webs between the trees and lurked watchfully for flies and wasps and unwary hands. Long-tailed hornets swarmed and buzzed among the grapes, threatening Vivian as she ran the gauntlet to and from her studio. Armies of ants in the patios burrowed and loosened flagstones. Occasionally a viper emerged from cover and slid along the path.

In the evenings, small bats came out to cull any flying insect the voracious swifts (now departed) had left for them. They flew through open windows and fluttered round and round the living room, squirting their urine onto treasured glass and silver, and easily evading John's furious swipes with an old squash racquet, (the 'bat bat'). Later large fruit bats flew in from hillside caves where they lived and bred, to raid fruit trees and spatter white-washed walls with their excrement as they circled and crashed from tree to tree. In the mornings, the night depredations of tree rats lay scattered beneath the trees, oranges and lemons neatly eaten out, leaving only the skins already filled with swarming ants. Much vaunted summer! The least attractive of the seasons, it was a time for occasional escapes from exasperation.

Happily there were plenty of opportunities for escape. The mountain range of folded limestone stretching away into the hazy distance demanded exploration. It was rich in geological conundrums to be pondered, and archaeological treasures to be discovered or revisited - perhaps a little Byzantine church set among great fig trees in a remote, deserted valley, or the ruins of a Crusader castle perched on a distant peak. The coast and the sea were no less inviting. Some miles away there were the remains of an ancient settlement beside a pebbled bay, where shards, mosaics and barnacled pots lay in the clear green water, and sometimes an arrowhead or an old anchor stone might be found. This was a favourite place to begin a day's excursion, and specially to enjoy with visiting friends, combing the beach for 'finds', gathering smooth round pebbles to be taken home for paper-weights, then swimming in the buoyant water to gaze through goggles at the quiet world beneath where striped and coloured fish abounded among sea urchins and the swaying seaweeds.

At about midday, thirsty for cold beer and ready for lunch, it would be time to drive into the mountains to join Nicos at a shady forest station where he would be preparing long skewers of his delicious suvla. After a lively lunch, the last objective for the day-would usually be Kantara castle, the eastern-most bastion of the island's northern defence line in the times of the Crusades. The long steeply twisting road led through forests thronged with singing birds. High above, great griffin vultures circled on the thermal currents, watchful for some easy prey at one of the many dangerous bends. Far below, glimpsed between the trees, coastal villages glinted white against the blue of sea and sky. At last, late in the afternoon, the road emerging from the forest came to its craggy summit, and there suddenly high and close stood Kantara castle, rising from massive rocks as if a natural extension of the mountain-top. Formidable and forbidding, steeply inaccessible to exposed assault, and everywhere protected by battlements and towers narrowly slit for the arrows of defending archers, it looked impregnable, though the garrisons within must have been vulnerable to long sieges denying them provisions.

A rough path led up the precipitous approach to the portcullised gate. Inside, steep steps rose to the top of the highest rampart, and to a view commanding in its scope, and magnificent in its enchantment. No sentry watching there could have failed to spy a hostile fleet approaching from the north across the wide expanse of sea, unless beguiled by other aspects of the all-embracing scene. The island spread below. To the east the panhandle peninsula stretched away, bare and narrow beneath the evening stratus clouds. westwards, the coast blazed in golden light against the setting sun. To the south a blue haze blanketed the land as though preparing it for sleep. Jackdaws, Alpine Swifts and small Wheatears flew from battlements to trees in the slowly fading light, decorating the tranquil sky with the tracery of their flight as they sought their roosts. Only the carrion seeking vultures still wheeling patiently above, brought to the imagination bloody battles fought there long ago.

There was never time enough to linger long in that lovely place, far from home. As the sun began to redden, there would just be time enough to race down from the heights to the sea again, for one last swim in the darkening water before the long drive back to Bellapais.

Though the summer months were happily relieved by such diversions, autumn was the longed-for season. It came usually in mid-September, sometimes heralded by a pair of Golden Orioles swooping and whistling between the trees, searching for the last ripe figs. But the true heralds of approaching autumn were migrating cranes, as infallible as the returning swifts and swallows announcing the arrival of spring. Late in the afternoons they would appear in the western sky, loudly honking to keep together in their ragged arrowhead formations, their slowly beating wings disguising the swiftness of their flight, the often changing leader betraying their exhaustion. String after string, they flew eastwards, till almost out of sight in less than a couple of minutes, they turned across the mountains to their distant winter destination in the south, leaving behind them a sure promise of the approaching end of summer.

Soon afterwards as the heat abated to the mild, warm days and cool crisp evenings of October, drowsy afternoons were stirred to life again. The hills beckoned with sharp edged views and changing skies. All was quiet there. The last of the cicadas had died upon the branches, and the only sounds to be heard were a shepherd's Pan pipes in the distance, the clonking of goat bells and now and again on the breeze, faint echoes of the abbey bell. In the village, other sounds betokened autumn, the thud of an axe against a tree to be cut for firewood, the rattling of pebbles in dry gourds to hollow them for wine flasks, the clip-clop of hooves on cobbled paths as donkeys brought in the last of the olive harvest.

Long hoped-for rains came sometimes in November, perhaps not till December, but when they did they came in torrents. Billowing black clouds sailed across the white-capped sea. Thunder rumbled and crackled, chasing lightning round the hills. Down came the rain, suddenly, relentlessly drumming on tiles and window panes. Every drop was welcomed by the villagers as they guessed the inches falling on dry fields.

For John and Vivian, winter was the favourite season of the year. Undisturbed, even comforted by the familiar rain and winds reminding them of Scotland, they found new impulse in the mornings. Imagination stirred. Ideas came to life again. In the evenings they sat before a sparking fire to discuss excitedly what they had done each day and what they would do on the next.

At night they often went to sleep to a strange but soothing lullaby. Over the garden wall there was a carob mill where a toffee made from carob beans was produced on winter nights. The scene inside the smoke-blackened mill room reminded them of a late Goya painting - one of the grotesque 'Black Goyas'. Sacks of carob beans were stacked along the walls. In the middle of the room there stood a massive annular trough in which the hard black pods were crushed to bran beneath a huge stone mill wheel, pulled round and round by a blindfolded donkey urged on by the mutterings and occasional shrieks of a fierce old woman dressed in dusty tatters. In a corner of the room over a roaring fire, there was a seething cauldron into which the bran was tossed, to be stirred all through the night by two large sweating men sharing an enormous wooden spoon. As they lay in bed, imagining the lofty smoke-filled room lit fitfully by the fire, listening to the rhythmic thumping of the spoon and the softly padding hooves on the earthen floor, John and Vivian soon fell asleep. In the mornings they were conveniently awakened at an early hour by the complaint of the exhausted donkey braying for its corn.

Almost imperceptibly the seasons passed, like a slowly changing backdrop to the unchanging scene of diurnal life ruled by the natural divisions of the the day, morning, afternoon and evening. Morning, the hub of the day was for work uninterrupted. Vivian worked confidently and quickly. At first, rooted in the traditions of the Paris School she used charcoal, pastel or oil paint for portraits, still-life and landscapes. But soon she began to feel the need of more exploratory approaches to picture making in a rapidly changing world. One day as she was painting a landscape, a jet plane zoomed suddenly overhead. The innocent scene had changed and with it the old conventional way of painting. She must catch up with the realities of the present and express them in quite new ways.

To this end she turned to the Sciences and read Chemistry, Physics, Biology, Geology, Relativity and Quantum theory, subatomic particle behaviour, Astronomy and Cosmology, seeking out the structures and principles of organic forms from the smallest leaf or crystal, molecule or atom, to the unimaginably vast galaxies. Here lay the fundamental truths at the very edge of advancing time and knowledge, somehow to be imagined and expressed with the freedom they demanded, and yet with understandable coherence. She must invent an abstract technique, and search for new materials.

She was not long in finding them. Opaque fragments of fractured glass from smashed car windscreens of which there was an abundant supply served perfectly for crystals, stars or galaxies, clear white mirror glass cut and set in three dimensions to reflect the eternal light of the universe, stained glass for prismatic light, shining sheet brass, bent and angled to catch imagined solar heat, and hot pigmented wax swiftly applied in whorls of blazing colour for exploding supernovae. In all her pictures, Vivian was the happy celebrator of her rapidly expanding new-found world.

John was not a celebrator. For some reason which he never quite understood, he was the reverse, perhaps because for him, music was above all an expression of feeling, and deep feeling is often tinged with sadness. Though he had studied the elements of composition, harmony and counterpoint, as assiduously as a busy life had allowed, unlike Vivian whose inventiveness in quick facility never failed her, he laboured slowly at his compositions, forever revising till he was satisfied with them. He wrote only songs. His gods were Schubert, Wolf, Duparc and Janacek. The poems he chiefly sought to set were those of his old friend Sydney Goodsir Smith the Scottish poet, and the Spanish poems of Federico Garcia Lorca. Their emotional content was paramount, clamouring for response in music. A picture implanted by the poem was always in his mind as he strove to translate it into expressive sound, the piano setting the prevailing or changing mood, the voice freely declaiming the words, each with its own independence, as might be imagined by a bird singing in a tree beside a calm or turbulent stream. At a vast distance, he struggled humbly but obsessed in the footsteps of the incomparable Masters, ever seeking a contemporary language of his own. Thus the mornings passed, John and Vivian totally absorbed in their separate pursuits.

Afternoons were for rest in the heat of summer, walks in the cooler weather, and afterwards whatever the season, for the collection of mail, the climax of the day. Late in the afternoon the postman, a villager returning from work, arrived in the square on his motor cycle with the mail he had picked up from the Post Office in Kyrenia. The mail bag was emptied onto the counter in Dimitri's coffee-shop, and the waiting villagers crowded in as Dimitri called out the names of the lucky ones and passed the letters to eager outstretched hands. But since his reading was limited to Greek, letters addressed to foreigners were put into a little box above the counter to be collected later.

For some years John and Vivian had had the box to themselves, the few other foreigners who later came to settle in the village, preferring to collect their mail in Kyrenia. Among the newcomers however there was one who chose to share the box with John and Vivian. 'Doc' Fraser (affectionately dubbed 'The little Doc' by the villagers), was a sturdy little Highlander. Though his hair was white he had the bouncing energy of a young man half his age. The old man's hearing aid he wore, fooled nobody. He could hear well enough without it when he wanted to. His eyes were alert and full of mischief. His mind was quick and he loved a lively argument, rational or irrational by turns, whichever best suited his attack, but constant in his convictions and Highland superstitions, the most implacable of which were that John and Vivian always and most unjustly received far more than their fair share of letters.

About half an hour after the village mail had been distributed, the little Doc would come bounding into the coffee-shop to meet John and Vivian for the ritual search of 'The Box'. A few pleasantries would be exchanged, and polite enquiries about each other's health. Then slowly filling his pipe with a show of confidence, and murmuring some observations about the current state of the world in which 'some people' got more than they deserved, the Doc would compose himself for the ordeal. When he was ready he would raise his eyes to the box on the shelf above the counter, and intone the opening prayer.

"Give us this day our daily mail."

"Who shall take the box down?" John would ask in ritual response.

"Who else but you dear boy. You're younger and stronger than I am. But use both hands. It'll be very heavy with all your ill-gotten letters. Be careful not to spill them."

"I think I can just manage it," John would say as he lifted the small box and put it lightly down onto the counter. As often as not the box was empty. All three would then console each other with sighs and muttered imprecations against Fate the common enemy.

At other times the box might be half filled, with mail for everyone in fairly equal shares, though since the odds were two to one in favour of John and Vivian, they usually did a little better than the opposition. The Doc would thump the counter and protest.

"Hogging it as usual. It's preposterous."

"You're very welcome to these thin buff envelopes," John might say. "The letters will begin 'Dear Sir/Madam' or perhaps 'Dear Sir unless...' Riveting in their way, but rather less exciting I suspect than those fat letters in scented envelopes addressed by an impassioned feminine hand which you've just pocketed with a furtive smile."

"You're more than kind," the Doc would murmur, "but I think for once I may indeed have a richer share."

The Doc's response was a good deal less urbane on the rare occasions when the box was filled with mail for John and Vivian. "You've swiped the lot. There ought to be a law!"

"Well, there's the Law of Averages. We come out pretty even in the end."

"Grrr!"

There was always an audience of old men seated round the walls to watch the entertainment. They could barely understand the words, but had no need to. The shrugs and frowns, the eyes and arms raised heavenwards in disbelief and supplication were eloquent enough. Doc was the star performer and often drew applause when he was observed in the heat of protestation, to be slyly stuffing a pocket with some of those fat letters. Nothing escaped the amused eyes of the old men as they watched and nudged each other at every gesture of triumph or defeat. But they must often have been puzzled when the three went out after furious debate to sit together laughing in the square.

Every year or two when her studio was filled to the door with pictures, Vivian had an exhibition. For a month or so, mornings and afternoons were given up to plans and preparations for the big event. On the first of these occasions, before they had become familiar, there were many unexpected problems to be dealt with.

Where was the exhibition to be held? There was a small unused building in the abbey grounds with a handsome arcaded veranda and several white-washed rooms which would be ideal for the purpose. They went to Costas Kollis to ask his permission as curator for its use.

"That's beyond my authority." Costas said. "You'll have to apply to the Minister of Communications and Works."

"But we're not asking for a telephone or any extensions to the building, just for the use of it as it is," said Vivian with a puzzled smile, "and if we have to go up the ladder, surely we should see the Director of Antiquities?"

"He's the Director of just one of the Minister's departments. Go and see the Minister. He's a very good man and interested in art."

The Minister listened patiently to Vivian's proposal. Why did she want to show her pictures in that particular place? There were several galleries in Nicosia. Her answers evidently met with his approval. Bellapais had become her home. She loved the village and all her pictures had been painted there. Where else would she want to show them but in that perfect setting beside the abbey? The Minister asked more questions, and soon he and Vivian were engaged in a lively conversation about modern painting in which, to Vivian's relief he was much interested. Telephones were ringing. The Minister had a busy day ahead. "Don't worry," he said. "You shall have your exhibition in that little building, and I shall come to open it. You'd better go and tell the Director of Antiquities. I'm sure he'll agree with my decision."

The Director was enthusiastic. "Anything that brings more visitors to the abbey has my support." he said. "We need their entrance fees to help pay for small repairs and the upkeep of the garden. I'm not much interested in modern painting, but I'll come to your show, and if you can pull a good crowd to it, perhaps I'll buy a picture." (In the event he did and took the best.) "Tell Costas that you have permission, and make your arrangements through him."

When Costas heard the news he beamed. "If the Minister is going to open the exhibition you can expect a lot of people and also press reporters and a television team. We'll need a policeman to direct the traffic. You can count on me to help in any way I can."

John and Vivian went up to the house and sat down to discuss the quite unexpected situation. John though somewhat awed by the turn of events, was relaxed and cheerful, but Vivian the realist was looking very thoughtful.
"Well everything seems to be arranged," John said airily. "Now I can get back to my work again."
"Not a hope. You're going to be very busy I'm afraid."
"But why?"

"I'd planned a simple show which you and I could manage easily together. Now that the Minister is to open it, we'll have to open with a Private View."

"Well that sounds quite simple, even cosy."

"It isn't. We'll have to invite lots of guests from the Embassies."

"That doesn't sound exactly private."

"No, and just listen to what you're going to have to do. You'd better brace yourself."

John hitched up his braces. "Shoot," he said with rather more attention. "I'm trying to be brave."

"Your first job will be to produce a list of guests with the help of our Embassy friends, maybe about a hundred."

"Steady!"

"Your second job will be to compose the invitation card and send out printed copies, all addressed correctly, in good time before the day. That'll keep you busy for a week or two I think."

John didn't disagree. "What else?" he murmured.

"Let's see. Oh the catalogues of course. You always have to have catalogues for the guests at a Private View."

"I do wish you wouldn't keep calling it *private*."

"So your third job will be to type the list of pictures with their titles and numbers, then have copies nicely printed."

John was absently drumming his fingers. Not counting numbers, but trying to catch a tune that had come into his head. "How many beats, I mean pictures?" he asked vaguely.

"Oh, about sixty I suppose."

"And how many copies of the catalogue?"

"Well, as the show is to continue for a week, we'd better have some spares, so let's say three hundred. And that reminds me..."

"Please no!"

"You'll have to type notices for the papers and shop windows, advertising the place, the time of day and the duration of the...er..."

"Public View? By then I'll be crippled with writer's cramp. Both hands paralysed. If you've any more ideas you can write me off as walking wounded."

"Cheer up," said Vivian "I've better news for you."

"Let's have it then. I need it."

"We'll have to find some helpers for the, er, Opening."

"You mean some other helpers? What are they going to do?"

"There must be someone at the door to check the invitation cards and hand out the catalogues. The little Doc perhaps?"

"Yes, yes."

"And someone in charge of the master catalogue, to record sales if any."

"The master catalogue? That sounds like me again."

"Well yes. Not in charge of it. You'll only have had to type it, and in rather more detail than the hand-out catalogues, but you'll be very familiar with them."

"Very." John's fingers stopped tapping out his tune. "If you've any more so-called better news, play the next bit softly, *una corda*, I implore you."

"We need a commanding person with a large red pencil to mark the pictures sold."

"A commanding person? Well that lets me out thank God."

"And we'll have to have plenty of wine and somebody who knows how to serve it. I thought of..."

"Anthimos of course. Well that seems to take care of everything," said John brightening a little.

"Just about everything for the opening day. For the rest of the week you and I can cope alone, one of us in the mornings and the other in the afternoons, to show people round."

Vivian paused for a moment. "There is one final trifling detail."

"Just whisper it. *Pianissimo*."

"The choosing of the pictures. Remember them? They're what the show is for! They have to be chosen, numbered and hung well-matched on each wall of the little rooms."

John conceded the point. "It calls for two committees. One for the selection, the other for the hanging. But let's just appoint ourselves for both."

The Joint Committee sat for several days over their deliberations, till at last they reached agreement. They then unanimously agreed that yet another helper should be engaged to take the sixty pictures down the hill. Both votes were for Andreas who brought his donkey to the gate and loaded it six times till all were safely delivered. For the next seven days while John laboured with stiff fingers over the catalogues, Vivian was hanging pictures and searching for her helpers. Costas, true to his promise, was attending to forgotten practicalities; a chair and a table for the Doc, a large trestle table and two clean sheets to cover it, for the wine, and a last minute appeal to the Police for a traffic officer.

All was ready just in time. The sun was shining and the day promised well, as John and Vivian went down to the abbey garden about an hour before the show was to be opened. The policeman was already on duty in the square. "God knows how many cars I'll have to park!" he said cheerfully. "Hope you sell as many pictures."

Costas emerging from his office by the gate was smiling happily. "I've brought an extra box for the entrance fees today." he said. In the shade of the veranda, Anthimos, white-jacketed, was pouring wine into rows of glasses.

"No rubbish I hope," said John.

"Not rubbish," said Anthimos. "All trash."

John sipped a glass and found it young but acceptable. "The word is *fresh* not *trash*," he said with much relief.

The Doc was sitting at his table outside the entrance door, surveying the pile of catalogues in front of him.

"Everything OK?" Vivian asked.

"Situation normal," he pronounced puffing at his pipe.

"Instead of your usual stack of letters I'm confronted with this heap of catalogues. Rather duller reading than your letters I imagine. If you've read one you've read the lot! What am I supposed to do with them?"

"Just hand them out to everyone who comes with an invitation card, as all our guests have been asked to do."

"What do I do if someone comes without an invitation card?"

"Well, some no doubt will forget to bring them. Others uninvited may just be attracted by the wine. But we don't want to turn any good people away. You'll have to use your much respected judgement."

"OK, I understand. A kindly word for one and all, but keep the rabble out!"

"That's rather too forbidding. We want everyone who may come, to enjoy themselves and hope they'll be more interested in the pictures than the wine."

Cars were beginning to arrive, and soon there was a growing crowd of guests, reporters, photographers and television men laden with heavy apparatus, all waiting for the Minister. He was late. Perhaps he had forgotten? After half an hour, people were glancing at their watches and becoming restive. The show would have to be opened before everyone drifted away in the wake of the television team which had already left. John explaining that the Minister had evidently been delayed, unlocked the door. The Doc woke from a restful doze, re-lit his pipe, and with a charming smile but a watchful eye for any unforthcoming invitation cards, handed out the catalogues and welcomed the guests inside. The Minister had not forgotten and eventually arrived. He had been held up by a committee meeting which refused to reach agreement. John and Vivian in full sympathy, mentioned their own disagreements as a joint committee of two.

They went inside, and walking slowly round, pausing here and there, John and Vivian soon noticed that there were red dots everywhere, spreading like a measles rash among the pictures. Suddenly the Minister bolted.

"What happened?" John asked. "What were you saying to him?"

"I was only explaining a picture."

They found him in a further room, standing in front of a picture which he'd just commanded the 'commanding person' to mark for him.

"Most of the best have been taken," he said. "If only I'd been here in time I'd have had the pick of them. But this is one I want."

All the pictures had been painted with molten wax which imposed a strict technique. Since the hot liquid wax cooled and solidified within a few seconds, each stroke had to be applied confidently and swiftly. This imparted life and spontaneity to the free linear designs in bold bright colour. No one had seen pictures such as these before, as Vivian herself had developed the medium and the method after much experiment. The guests were evidently attracted and intrigued by them.

After the first hour John counted twenty-eight red dots, and whispered the news to Vivian.

"It must be because of the wine!" she said bewildered.

"Well, *In vino veritas*!"

When all had departed, the measles had spread to an epidemic, with few pictures uninfected.

Afterwards, as John and Vivian sat over a lengthy lunch with all their happy helpers, John asked the Doc how he had managed at the door.

"Dropped a couple of clangers I'm afraid. Two chaps turned up without their invitation cards..."

"They'd just forgotten them? So what?"

"Well, with a kindly smile I asked the first if he could identify himself. 'I think I can', he said."

"Who was he?"

"The High Commissioner."

John gulped his glass of wine and filled it up again.

"What about the second chap, could he identify himself?"

"Yes. He said 'I thought perhaps you might have recognised me as Chief Advisor to the Head of State.'"

"Loud, resounding clangers. But I'm sure you were able to explain."

"I did my best, and they were very nice and understanding. Kindly words were exchanged as I meekly bowed them in."

The next six days were less eventful. More people came and showed interest, but there were only a few small pickings left unsold. At the end of the week, after the new owners had collected their pictures and taken them away, John and Vivian went lightly up the hill with the remainder.

"Well, despite the sweated labour I must admit that the Private View was worth it. It was the saving of the show." said John.

"I suppose so," Vivian said "if you're counting the pictures sold, but all I really care about is that whether sold or not people should just like my pictures."

John thought about that for a moment. He was humming his new tune. "And all I care about," he said, "is that I should like my songs." They smiled together in understanding disagreement.

After these disrupting interludes, John and Vivian soon settled down again to their busy mornings, the relaxations of the afternoons, and to the evenings whatever or whoever they might bring. Evening had always been the time for visitors, even in the early years during holidays from Arabia, before they had retired. In those days there had not been many.

Lawrence Durrell who had bought a house nearby, had been the first. He was a warm and generous neighbour, helping John and Vivian when his impeccable Greek was needed, and never passing the gate on his way down the hill to his car, without offering a lift. Once when Vivian and Deirdre were in the village on holiday together, he found them sitting forlornly in the square. Vivian had just brought Deirdre back from the Kyrenia hospital where she had spent a week, acutely ill. Now recovered she was still too weak to walk up to the house. So he took her gently up the hill on donkey-back, amusing her with stories on the way.

He liked to mask his prodigious gifts of sensibility and intellect with a teasing sense of humour. One day, standing in the garden for a moment to talk with Vivian, his eyes strayed to the head of the Apollo in the middle of the pond. A few minutes later John was called to see how it had been improved by a touch of colour. The eyes were blue, the lips were red. John was furious as expected, thinking they'd been painted. Then with a wink at Vivian and a disarming smile to John, he peeled off the blue and red flower petals.

Whenever he came into the house he enlarged it with his brilliant talk; perhaps a hilariously embellished account of some small incident which had happened during the day, or a dissertation upon any subject which occurred to him, fluently expounded from deep knowledge, and lit with shafts of his lightning imagination. He was an irrepressible force, a spellbinder who could capture a roomful of people and reduce them to gasping laughter or to enchanted silence. When he had come to the village to stay for a few brief years, he had already written 'Prospero's Cell', 'Reflections on a Marine Venus' and much else which had set him on his way to fame, but not yet 'Bitter Lemons' which was to change the village and leave his imprint indelibly upon it.

That had been long ago. Some ten years later, cheap new package flights were bringing large numbers of tourists to the island, and many attracted by 'Bitter Lemons' were coming to the village. Tourism was booming and Bellapais was getting its full share, welcomed by some of the villagers who were profiting by it but with less enthusiasm by those who just wanted the village to remain unchanged. The newly awakened interest in the village brought not only fleeting tourists who at that time came for brief visits and then departed, but others drawn by a deeper impulse who returned to stay. They bought old houses and restored them, thus saving some of them from falling into ruin, brought some small prosperity to the villagers, adapted themselves to village customs, and were soon accepted as 'co-villagers' as the Muchtar benignly dubbed them.

They came from many walks of life, joined by the enchantment of the still unspoiled and lovely village, seeking houses for holidays and perhaps later for retirement. A few were working with the United Nations Development Programme for the island, (UNDP). Some came from busy city lives in England, Scotland or Cyprus. Two had left a farming life in Kenya. There were others, still active or retired from academic or professional careers. It was a serene and happy chapter while it lasted, villagers and co-villagers sharing the village harmoniously together in a long and seemingly unending summer of contentment. But no summer lasts forever. After twelve unclouded years, changes in the village and elsewhere in the island were to bring it to an end. The newcomers though by then rooted in the life and fabric of the village one by one began to leave. Except for a very few who chose to stay, and others who have kept their houses and sometimes come to visit, all now have gone. But their remembered presences remain, especially those of close friends and neighbours.

Dr. Earl Hald, a professor of Economics and the Director of UNDP, tall, reflective and very able, with his brilliant young wife Margery, also an economist, had been the first to take a house and convert it to their needs and comforts. There, before a log fire in the winter, or outside in the garden on summer evenings, John and Vivian would sit with them over sumptuous suppers prepared by Margery with no noticeable notions of economy, and afterwards would join in lively, sometimes rather less than coolly argued disputation upon any subject that might occur to them, Earl the wise and chuckling arbiter deftly teasing it along, and when the talk became too tangled or collapsed in laughter, gently dousing it with some brooding music of Sibelius which subdued all argument and sent everyone contentedly to bed.

Jack and Betty Burbidge, the first to settle as close neighbours, bought and re-built a ruined house above Irini. Jack, a UNDP lecturer in Production Management, already looked like the professor he was later to become. He had a large impressive presence and an air of near-sighted absent-mindedness which with sly humour it amused him to pretend, endearing him to his friends and deceiving no one acquainted with his sharply observant and deeply thoughtful mind. Betty, a practising medical doctor, quickly decisive, fearlessly independent was quite the opposite in temperament. Athletic, practical, undaunted by any emergency, she was the embodiment of active cheerful life. Each was the perfect foil for the other. They came often in the evenings to Irini, Betty with quick steps, Jack following in his slippers, absent-mindedly or perhaps presciently, carrying a half-finished glass of wine which would need to be replenished as they swapped ideas and news amidst much laughter till the sun went down and the moon came up.

James Pickering bought another house nearby, and came for short visits from a busy life in England. Slight of build, massive in mind, he was a polymath and a man of many accomplishments, not the least of which were his brilliant contributions to archaeology by aerial surveys of ancient field patterns in rural England, from a helicopter which he piloted himself. There seemed to be no subject beyond his interest or grasp, no situation which escaped his understanding. Words and wisdom spiced with laughter flew from brain to tongue sometimes faster than the tongue could manage. He was deeply attached to the village and the villagers, the simplicities of life of no less concern to him than the complexities. He was a sprightly effervescent spirit whose visitations were events to be remembered.

Ken and Claire Luard had come to the island from Kenya, and soon discovering Bellapais, decided to put new roots down there. Close beside the abbey they found a rambling old house with a large neglected garden. They bought it, ingeniously planned and handsomely restored the house. In the sprawling long-untended garden, among wilting trees and thriving weeds, two tall date palms and an ancient mulberry still sturdily survived. Round this nucleus, with unrelenting work and much imagination, the garden was slowly coaxed to life. Water in abundance came tumbling over a rocky waterfall. In place of weeds, trim lawns appeared. Drooping trees held up their heads again. Shrubs and flowers planted in profusion, celebrated the rejuvenation of a dying garden into a little Eden.

Ken, a versatile engineer and builder, was to be the rejuvenator of many old houses in the village, providing them with modern plumbing and rebuilding with discreet additions in the traditional village style. Claire, when the garden had been established, turned her energies and her searching mind to another challenging ambition, a deep study of English Literature which she pursued with joyful zeal. John and Vivian, sharing their enthusiasms, shared also their warm friendship for some ten years till they moved on to other beckoning horizons, leaving behind them a continuing reminder of their presence: 'Abbey House' with the enchanting garden they had created, was soon after their departure taken over as an elegant restaurant. A lasting contribution to the village.

Simon Gordon-Duff, another helicopter pilot, took a small house near Irini, and came from the British Bases at weekends and on longer leaves to relax on terra firma. A red-haired, sturdy and very capable young man of a lively disposition, he soon made many friends among the villagers including John and Vivian. His mind was open and receptive to new experiences outside his life as a pilot, such as unfamiliar music to which he listened with enthusiasm in Irini. He also quickly took to Vivian's unusual pictures. For their part, John and

Vivian unfamiliar with the mysteries of the improbable looking flying machine he flew with evident confidence, pestered him with questions about rotating wings and their management, especially should rotary motion cease unexpectedly! From his modest, smiling answers they concluded that he was a most intrepid and resourceful pilot. Cool head. Warm heart. The red hair, strong build, easy laughter and an often expectant eye, suggested an exuberance awaiting an occasion which from time to time he himself memorably provided. With two chefs in attendance to carve and serve, great roasts would be dispensed with abundant wine to the guests overfilling his small house but never exhausting their exuberant welcome. Sadly, but inevitably in the course of duty, he left the island. When he came to say goodbye he brought with him a rare and much treasured book about Beethoven the Man, whose music had deeply stirred him.

Maxwell and Lillan Harper Gow, (now Sir Maxwell and Lady Harper Gow) on holiday from Edinburgh where Max was Chairman of a famous whaling company, came up to Bellapais one sunny morning, and while wandering round the village discovered the carob mill over the wall from Irini. It was old and grimy, the walls encrusted with soot, and dust from the unpaved floor, the only living accommodation a few small rooms beside it. Outside there was a large hen-run of hard bare earth. Despite the manifest deficiencies, they were much taken by its character and quiet isolation. They bought it and with unobtrusive additions transformed it into a spacious holiday house, keeping the old mill room as a large and handsome living room.

The crowning transformation was the planting of the hen-yard, a bleak wilderness overlooked from the windows of Irini. Steve the village cobbler, was the magician who agreed to tackle the seemingly impossible. As familiar with the local soil as he was with leather, as deft with trowel or secateurs as with thread and needle, he was also intuitive and wise, knowing what would grow and what would not. Everything he planted thrived. The view from all windows is now a riotous garden of flowers and climbing plants in a small forest of orange, lemon and jacaranda trees over-topped by tall swaying cypresses.

For twelve years or more, Max and Lillan came on their annual holidays, always lively occasions joyfully shared by John and Vivian. Max, a tall commanding figure in his middle age, at the peak of a demanding and adventurous career which had taken him three times to his company's whaling station in Antarctica, looked a good deal younger than his years. Energetic and ready for any adventure, he enjoyed his life with youthful zest. Lillan, open-hearted, warmly welcoming, shared his appetite for life with spontaneous generosity. During one of Vivian's exhibitions in the garden, it was Lillan who secretly prepared and brought a delicious lunch to sustain everyone at a lull in the proceedings. After a long day together in the mountains, it would be Lillan, however weary, who produced a supper over lively talk in the great mill room.
In that generous house, friendship grew as naturally as the garden richly flourishing outside. Close neighbours and ever closer friends, alas now long departed from the village.

Doc Fraser who arrived at about that time, had retired from his practice in the Highlands, seeking a warmer climate in some quiet place where he could pursue his natural talents as a potter. He found both in Bellapais, and industriously at his wheel, (happily never in anger!) 'threw' pots and jugs and bowls, cups and mugs and goblets, beautifully turned and shaped, many of which are treasured and used daily in Irini.

All these had found old houses in the heart of the village or within its upper limit and had settled as near or immediate neighbours. Others among the first to come those many years ago; James and Dorothy Jowett, Michael and Dora Phillips, Chris and Yulie Phylactou, built their own new houses on the outer fringes of the village. No less close in friendship though not so often seen. Some of those who came and went, rented their houses during their longer absences to a further generation of newcomers.

Lawrence Durrell's house after his departure was soon occupied again. Penelope Tremayne spent some months there while writing her book 'Below the Tide', a vivid account of her experiences as a Red Cross worker elsewhere in the island during violent troubles which were still echoing to her endangerment even in the remote seclusion of the abbey square. The house was later bought by Ulla Ryghe, a film editor for Ingmar Bergman, who came on holidays from her busy life, drawn ever more closely to the village, the villagers and their daily lives in fields and houses. During one of her longer visits she decided to record it all in a film under her own direction. The film was produced and is still shown from time to time. It remains for John and Vivian who briefly appeared in it, a nostalgic reminder of the village as it was in its early innocence.

When Ulla left soon afterwards in the pursuit of her career, the house was let for several years to three young people from the British High Commission who brought their dazzling talk and warm companionship to Irini, Elizabeth Wallwyn, Stanley Duncan and John Griffiths of fond memory.

Jack and Betty Burbidge also let their house to others no less eagerly welcomed. They were Bureau Chiefs for Time and Newsweek Magazines, and came from Beirut and Jerusalem where they were stationed, as often as their hectic lives allowed, bringing their wives, their lively children and their own irrepressible exuberance, Marsh and Pippa Clark, Gavin and Sue Scott, Loren and Nancy Jenkins. For three happy years they came with their news and views, and their forthright opinions upon the products of Irini. Their pronouncements upon which were never less than frank, though not always to the point. Marsh abominated singers. Listening to one of John's songs he would mutter, "The piano part is OK, but I wish you'd leave that croaker out." When John objected that a song required a singer, he once replied, "Well Mendelssohn got it right. He wrote songs without words. No croaker!"

Vivian's pictures fared much better. Bold colour and design assert themselves with no need of words, croaked or spoken. All were enthusiastic, and whenever they left, they took away the pictures by the armful.

Two later arrivals among the permanent settlers were Iain and Fabienne Harrison who took one of the last remaining houses above Irini and then the long abandoned house just beside the gate, built by Andreas for Vassilia and their family. Old associations now renewed with life, theirs when they are here, and in their absences with the lively occupation of new found friends from the American Embassy.

So, after long digression, to return to the evenings in Irini. With the arrival of new co-villagers and others on their holidays, the evenings became enlivened with not a few, but many visitors. Friends and friends of friends on package tours from England, came drifting up the hill to sit and talk over a glass or two of wine. The vin was ordinaire, but the evenings were sometimes vintage.

Sir Michael Tippett[1] came one summer with two close friends, Eric Walter White and Karl Hawker, to spend a few weeks in Kyrenia. At the suggestion of a mutual friend in London they rang John and Vivian who invited them to supper a few days later. It was a sweltering evening in mid August, very hot and humid and without the faintest stirring of a breeze. They sat in the patio sipping long cold drinks which did little to cool them or replace their dripping sweat. As a little breeze sprang up, the general morale rose visibly.

They all sat down to supper round Charalambos's festive table, and as the evening cooled and the chilled wine circulated, the conversation flowed warmly, led by Eric White now fully in possession of his natural fluency. As Literary Director of the

British Council, poet, and author of authoritative books upon the lives and works of Stravinsky and Benjamin Britten, (much later he was to write another about Sir Michael), he discoursed easily upon many themes, literary and musical. Soon everyone was chipping in, and the circle came alive as the talk expanded and digressed. Karl Hawker, a gifted painter, teased it away from the particular to speculations about the Arts in general and their inter-relationships. Amiable discussion warmed further into vigorous debate, into which Vivian tossed a few explosive darts to keep it lively. Sir Michael, the quietly thoughtful and dominating presence at the table, amused by some of Vivian's bold sallies, joined in the fray to break a lance or two with her. But to John he spoke almost only of his astonished admiration for the young and greatly gifted music students he had taught at Morley College, with never a mention of his own immense achievements. A humbling, inspiring occasion despite its unpromising beginning.

They came again to relax and talk less strenuously on cooler evenings over a glass of wine, and once to look at some of Vivian's pictures. After their last visit, Sir Michael went away with a bright brass picture, a small echo perhaps, Vivian hoped, of the horns and trumpets in his triumphant scores.

On another summer evening Humphrey Searle and his wife Fiona came up to the house. They had rung to say that they were on holiday in Kyrenia, and mentioned a mutual friend. Perhaps they could arrange to meet? Of course. John tried to remember all he'd read and heard about the great man's prodigious gifts, composer of symphonies, concertos, operas and ballets, Professor of Composition at the Royal College of Music, adviser to Sadler's Wells and the BBC, author of many treatises and books, one of which, 'Twentieth Century Counterpoint' John had wrestled with, and wondered with much apprehension whether the man himself would be as formidable as his works.

---

[1] Sir Michael Kemp Tippett (1905-1998), English composer who rose to prominence during and immediately after the Second World War.

He need not have worried, at least not on that account. The tall spare figure with the massive brow who appeared in the patio was shy and diffident. He murmured a few words as he shook hands, then relapsed into abstracted silence. Beside him in vivid contrast, stood the beautiful raven-haired Fiona, lively and vivacious. But for her, that first meeting might have ended as it began, with scarcely a word exchanged. Drinks were produced, with the usual exploratory send-ups - how were they enjoying sunny Cyprus and so forth? Lead balloons! The silence deepened. How to break it? In desperation, John was emboldened to venture some questions about contemporary composers and current trends in composition. The tense figure gradually relaxed, and coaxed by Fiona, words began to flow, slowly at first, then in torrents as more eager questions followed.

In his young days he had studied with Webern and Janacek, both at the very growing edge of the New Music where his own deep interest lay. He spoke with affection of Constant Lambert and Peter Warlock whom he had known in their brilliant short-lived hey-day and of others at that time, and was familiar with the works of his contemporaries, old and young, everywhere, especially those of the most adventurous among the rising generation. He talked quickly and incisively from vast knowledge and experience, but such was his self-effacing diffidence that he had to be constantly rescued from sudden silences. Fiona, his beguiling and persuasive prompt, coaxed and teased till he seemed to be at ease as a gentle smile appeared. The spell at last was broken. The evening opened.

A few days later they returned. Vivian had prepared supper for them in the patio, but they had already eaten. Fiona ate two strawberries. It didn't matter. John and Vivian fed on Humphrey's now fluent talk and reminiscences and his lighter enthusiasms which turned by chance to the Marx Brothers. The last remaining barrier to his reticence dissolved. The rest of the evening was spent in explosive laughter.

A day or two before they left, Humphrey took a few of John's songs away to look at. On their last evening he and Fiona came back to return them and say goodbye. That morning they had waited in the crowded foyer of their hotel till it had emptied of small boys bouncing footballs, and Humphrey had been able to hear the songs as he went through them at the old piano there. John, expecting the scores to be returned with a few embarrassed and dismissive words, was astonished and delighted when Humphrey nodded his approval. Fiona on her part had been much taken by a setting of a Lorca poem dedicated to Deirdre, so John added Fiona to the dedication as his 'adopted daughter'. During their short stay, the first of many further meetings, John and Vivian had become devoted to them both. Beneath his extreme reserve, they had discovered in Humphrey a depth of warm and gentle kindness, and in Fiona they had found an adorable 'adopted' daughter.

Alexander Goehr[1] came for a brief but long remembered visit during a short stay in the village. John knew him by reputation as a fast-rising composer of the younger generation, had heard a little of his music, and from his occasional writings had some small acquaintance with his brilliant eclectic mind. He had studied at the Royal Manchester College of Music (RMCM) and later with Messaien, and had been a protégé of Tippett. In his works he made much use of serialism while accepting that traditional harmonic and contrapuntal procedures still had a place in the new approaches to composition. Highly original and innovative yet tolerant in his views, he had just been appointed to the Chair of Music at Leeds University.

The stockily built, warm and friendly young man John met, was cheerful and relaxed. Soon they were engaged in easy conversation which turned naturally from generalities to music and the contemporary scene. At one point John produced a record, Three Pieces (for piano) by Alexander Goehr. "Just to show you that your music has reached even sleepy Bellapais where the plain chant still prevails."

It was a happy impulse. The Three Pieces, despite the disarming title were far from simple. They were played by the already legendary John Ogdon, a close friend of Ronald Stevenson the protean composer, pianist and musicologist who had tutored John in Composition. Both had studied at the RMCM, and the talk thus connecting, led inevitably to the other two immensely gifted members of the Manchester School, Peter Maxwell Davies and Harrison Birtwistle, who were opening and exploring new territories of sound in great imaginative works. The conversation blazed as Alexander fuelled and kept it sparkling with speculative ideas and fluent answers to puzzled questions. "How did you imagine and write down these new and complex sounds, often with no anchorage in a scale or mode, just twelve slippery semitones?" John asked in naive perplexity. The answer as he vaguely understood it, seemed to be that you just conceived them and adjusted them to the structure as it grew. Quite!

John envied the young music students at Leeds as he imagined them, released to new hard-won horizons under the visionary tutelage of their newly appointed Professor. A few weeks after that most happy and absorbing meeting, a copy of the score of Alexander's fourth opera, *Arden Muss Sterben* (Arden Must Die) arrived, a much treasured memento of his visit.

Summer was the usual season for visitors, but one crisp autumn evening Vivian went to the door in answer to a gentle knock. There stood Hephzibah Menuhin[1] and her husband Richard Hauser. They were visiting the island on behalf of the Institute of Social Research, of which Richard Hauser was the Director, to attend a conference in Nicosia for the Promotion of Peace by the Women of the World. But alas the women at the meetings had been unable to reach any peaceable agreement about how this might be done, so they had slipped away for a few hours to seek peace in Bellapais.

---

[1] Alexander Goehr (born 1932),

English composer and academic.

As they came into the room they brought their own peace with them, Hephzibah a small and vivid figure, bright-eyed and smiling, Richard Hauser gravely benign. They spoke lightly and amusingly about their first impressions of the island which they were much enjoying despite the disagreements at the conference. Hephzibah, alert and lively, sat looking round the room. Once or twice she glanced at the piano with enquiring interest, but her eyes kept returning to Vivian's pictures on the walls. Soon she and her husband were walking about discussing them with Vivian, who explained her method, using molten wax, powdered pigments and gold leaf. They wanted to see more, so Vivian took them to her studio to show them what was there, and after quick deliberation they chose two to take back with them to London.

The evening had begun briskly and surprisingly. The serenity, evident at once in each of them as they arrived, far from passive was very much alive. Richard Hauser's initial gravity was soon unmasked as he smiled and talked with gently mordant wit. Hephzibah was translucently her shining natural self as they sat in the house again. She had further surprises to announce. Her daughter, a young aspiring painter seeking new and free approaches such as Vivian had found, would surely find a needed stimulus when they showed her the pictures they had chosen. If so, perhaps she might come to Bellapais and work with Vivian for a month or two? Of course, said Vivian. They could exchange ideas, each learning from the other. An exciting proposition. Another closely followed. Swift decisions seemed to be natural to them both.

Their first glimpse of the village had already decided them to return for a holiday in the summer, if their very busy lives and Hephzibah's commitments to concerts and recitals should allow. Bellapais, sleeping in ancient peace beneath the abbey, without benefit of conferences, drew them irresistibly. Where could they stay? Their time was short, and they were eager to make arrangements before they left the island.

---

[1] Hephzibah Menuhin (1920-1981), American-Australian pianist, writer, and human rights campaigner.

"Let's all have lunch tomorrow in the square and then explore," said Vivian

Next day over lunch the mood was jubilant. With the *mezzes*, wine was offered, but John and Vivian suspecting that the other two drank none, hesitated in a moment of unusual indecision.

"Don't be shy!" said Hephzibah with much amusement as she ordered a bottle of the best.

Their plans for the summer and their daughter's hoped-for visit were excitedly discussed, but the ineluctable question upon which all depended was now of chief concern. Where could they stay?

"Just a simple little village house is all we'd need," said Hephzibah.

"And a piano perhaps?" said John "Mine would be tuned and ready whenever you might want to use it." The prospects were enchanting, but the chances of finding an empty house were slim as John and Vivian, at first optimistic, more thoughtfully considered them. The villagers scarcely ever went away. Vivian busily thinking, made a note of two or three which might be possibilities. "Let's explore," she said.

The rest of the afternoon was spent with fading hopes, searching and enquiring. Doors were opened in welcome, *glikes* were produced. There was much cheerful chat, but the answers to the crucial question were all the same. The house was always full and not 'to let'. So nothing came of either plan and the following day they would leave the island, and though letters were exchanged John and Vivian would never see them again or meet their daughter. As they drove away, John and Vivian waved a sad goodbye, and Hephzibah turning in her seat, cheerfully waved back. Their vivid presence in the village had been just a fleeting glimpse, but John and Vivian would never forget that zestful little figure with the sturdy pianist's shoulders and strong small hands, her quick and joyful smile.

Such occasions and others associated with visitors, expeditions to the mountains and the sea, feasts of good talk and food and wine, meetings with old friends bringing news and new ideas, were both stimulating and relaxing. Afterwards John and Vivian returned invigorated and refreshed, to their happily reclusive lives. The wheel of time moved slowly, paced by the natural rhythms of the days and seasons. For twelve long blissful years and more, Time itself had seemed to nod and sleep, so unchanging was the village, its unhurried life. Only the abbey bell, pealing and appealing, reminded Time to shake itself awake. It would have been better left to sleep and dream in peace. Sad changes and much trouble lay ahead.

JOHN GUTHRIE

Part II

JOHN GUTHRIE

PRELUDE

The villagers pursue their tranquil lives, obedient to the sovereign sun, heedful of the abbey bell which tolls for the dead and for dying summers soon to be obliterated from memory by destructive winter storms. To the very old the tolling bell foretells their own approaching deaths. Such natural events are accepted by young and old with gentle resignation, even mortal death which has lightly touched them all their nights with blessed sleep.

But their sleep is to be violently disrupted by harsh invasive changes in the village, waking them not to the simple expectations of their uneventful days but with growing apprehensions, to the end of them. The bell hangs muted in the belfry, only to be heard in faint undertones, stirred by a sighing breeze.

TOLLS

The bell tolls for deaths and the ends of fruitful days, telling, tolling and hesitating before the last full stop, as evening fades to night.

As the year advances on its round, the circle of the graveyard slowly fills. Here in the quiet village it is only the old who die. In the arena it is the young, thrusting with swords and lances, staking a life for a life. The only swords and lances here are the shadows of sentinel cypresses cast criss-cross and still across the grassy mounds.

Days draw in towards the winter solstice. Trees struggle with the wind. Lightning unzips the distant darkness. Thunder crackles and explodes. Rain drums on leaves in empty gardens. A thickly threaded curtain veils the hill. The curtain sags, tearing a hole in the sky. Through the rift a rainbow glistens in another world of half-forgotten sunlight. Swirling clouds race in. The gardens lie abandoned beneath relentless rain.

In the last thin sunlight of the day, old men sit at chequer boards round the abbey square. The darkening hill above them plunges down against the evening sky like the lowered neck of some huge stalking animal, its shadow crawling slowly, slyly forward. The old men drag their tables out of reach. The hunter follows. The old men move again. Steadily the black and white of shade and sun and chequer boards dissolves to grey. Shade and substance vanish in the fading light.

The bell tolls for sunset as the spent old sovereign sinks behind the hill. Women sit sewing on their doorsteps waiting for their men. The men come riding mules and donkeys, bringing loaves and bundled firewood. Voices rise and fall, then murmur into silence. One by one the shutters close. The village sighs and yawns and returns to sleep.

HANGS SILENT

The bell hangs silent. The village lies empty, silent and abandoned. There is no cock crow, no footstep on the flagstones in the mornings. No donkeys bray or clip-clop on the cobbles. No water whispers in the aqueducts. No children play and call to each other in the gardens. No neighbours murmur over supper in the evenings.

The houses are all closed and shuttered. In the silent streets no movement stirs, except perhaps for a scrap of wind-blown paper, a stray cat foraging among abandoned refuse, or a shutter swinging in the breeze. The abbey square is a wilderness of empty chairs and tables.

The village is silent, not with the quietness of peaceful life. The silence is unquiet because no life remains within the village.

No bell tolls for the hosts of vanished friends and memories.

The village is deserted. The abbey bell hangs silent.

THE BELL TOLLS

Someone once said that a story should be full of contrasts, as natural as light and shade. But that is not how this story is remembered. So far, all has been light, with scarcely a shadow cast as the village basked at its high noon, serene and undisturbed. Now the shadows insidiously begin to creep, grey at first then darkening with events.

The first bus-loads of tourists had arrived for brief visits in the mornings and departed leaving no trace upon the village. But with every year their numbers had swollen steadily to a surging flood. To the bus-loads in the mornings there were added as many more in the afternoons and evenings who came by car and stayed to linger in the square over drinks and what small snacks Dimitri was able to produce, a few peanuts and simple *mezzes*. Here was a horde of eager customers waiting to be captured.

To meet their growing demands, a restaurant was built opposite Dimitri's coffee shop to provide more tempting fare. It was named 'The Tree of Idleness', after a venerable old tree beneath which the old village men sat dozing for much of the day.

(Costas Kollis had given the tree its name, and later Lawrence Durrell had used it as the title for a book of poems).

The Tree of Idleness not only held the tourists longer on their visits, soon it was attracting local people not otherwise drawn to the village, to come and eat there. After a year or two it had become so crowded that the original building was pulled down and on the same site a very much larger one was built and filled.

But there was still room for competition. Another restaurant and bar appeared beside it, and the beautiful old arcaded school house was converted into yet another. Old houses round the square were taken over as souvenir shops. The much changed square and the narrow streets were choked with traffic. Many of the tourists after a cursory glance at the abbey, or just a snapshot taken from a car, swarmed into the restaurants and shops. Scantily clad young women queueing for entry to the abbey church, were turned away with a few sharp words from Costas Kollis. The Muchtar scowled and muttered about 'rascals'. In the evenings the Tree of Idleness filled with strangers singing foreign songs to the applause of shouts and strident whistling. Blaring motor horns added to the cacophony drowning the subdued and natural village sounds. The Tree of Idleness had virtually supplanted the abbey as the centre of the village. When centuries ago the abbey had fallen into decay, it had crumbled gracefully and slowly, still nourishing the village rising from its fallen stones from which many of the old houses had been built. Now the pace and face of change was of quite another kind. It was too sudden, alien and overwhelming for the village to absorb, bringing only noise and litter, congestion to the quiet streets, disruption in place of ancient peace.

The change continued in another way. As the tidal wave of tourists persisted unabated, an ever-increasing demand arose for building sites. It was met with a ready response among the villagers, many of whom owned plots of land inherited from their parents, and naturally enough were happy to sell at steeply rising prices.

New houses sprang up on the outskirts, adding no enchantment to the entrancing distant view. Then a holiday village appeared on the mountain-side above them, and saved it just in time. Shining white among trees and gardens, it seemed as though self-seeded, a natural growth discreetly distanced and bringing much relief to the old mother village under siege.

The idea caught on. Two more villa villages were planned. Unhappily the chosen site was a round green grassy hill, a lone treasured view at the edge of the old village. The hill was bulldozed and the houses were half built when troubles erupted in the island and put a halt to them. There the skeletons of the villas stand on the scarred and dusty hillside, a sad and perhaps permanent defacement of the lovely surrounding landscape.

In the midst of these disturbing changes, without warning, literally out of the sky, there occurred a devastating event which brought havoc to the village.

"April is the cruellest month." Fickle, unpredictable and sometimes savage. 'The April of the storm' was to be recorded as the worst for forty years. A black depression blanketed the island. For three weeks rain poured down in torrents, drumming on roof tiles, hissing along the streets, spouting from every drainpipe. Gardens were flooded and ruined, and many old houses were battered almost beyond repair. Walls collapsed and rooves fell in.

During the first violent downpour, water swirled into a house above Irini and swept away the owner's life-savings kept in bank notes underneath his bed. Next day the sun broke through the clouds for an hour or two, and the villagers turned out to help search for them. All the notes were miraculously retrieved, caught on rocks and shrubs and trees, and were later to be seen pegged to a clothes line, hanging out to dry. Was this perhaps an omen? John and Vivian joined in the general rejoicing with good hopes that the heavens might have decided to relent.

They hadn't. The clouds closed in and settled. The rain came down in solid sheets and continued without mercy day and night. Beneath the hammering noise, another sound, like thunder. But it wasn't thunder. It was too steadily rising and continuous. As they stood one morning listening outside the door, the answer came to them all too loud and clear. The sound was coming from the stream below the garden cliff Usually no more than a gentle trickle, it had risen to a roaring spate, tumbling rocks and boulders brought down from the ravaged hill-side.

"I must go and see what's happening," said John.

"Well, mind the puddles," said Vivian handing him his gumboots.

When he looked out from the gate John saw a bewildering and alarming scene. Above and to his left, the swollen stream thundered down and hurtled past the cliff. That was as expected. But straight ahead and quite separate from the stream, there was a broad, deep river rushing down the hill path, tossing on its surface forty-gallon oil drums, beams and poles and other debris from houses on the steeper slopes above. A few yards beyond the gate there was a dip in the path below a large and solid limestone rock protecting the gate and diverting the water to join the stream along the cliff. But if the river continued to rise it would soon fill the dip and race through the open tracery of the wrought-iron gate, which was useless as a barrier, flood the garden and inundate the house.

As John splashed back again trying to puzzle out the reason for this new river, it suddenly occurred to him. There was a dam high up on the hill which must have overfilled with rain and burst.

"It's the dam," he announced to Vivian.

"The damn what?"

John explained. "There's a raging Amazon heading for the gate. Unless we can stop it there, it'll soon be in the house. We must put up some sort of barricade."

Vivian who had been calmly waiting for bad news, put on an old red raincoat and picked up a tattered parasol.

"Well let's go and see what we can do," she said.

"What we need is a door." said John. "Do we have an old one we could use?"

"No, but there's an old shutter somewhere in the studio."

"That'll have to do," said John as they hurried along the path. "We'll bolster it up with stones against the gate."

They found the shutter and took it to the gate. It fitted well enough and there were plenty of stones and rocks conveniently delivered by the river, close to hand. Vivian was scarcely listening as she stood gazing at the plunging water.

"Oh how I'd love to paint it..."

"Some other time. From memory. You're not likely to forget it. We must build up the barricade. If you'll make a start I'll go and get some help. We need men with spades."

It was Good Friday, and all the village men were in Dimitri's coffee shop, snug and dry as they sat at cards and tric-trac. There seemed little chance of persuading anyone to leave. John turned to a likely looking man standing inside the door.

"My house is about to be flooded..." he began.

"When?"

"Perhaps within an hour."

The man smiled reassuringly. "Then you've time for a glass of wine," he said, drawing up a chair.

Someone sitting at a nearby table produced another equally less practical suggestion. "Call the Police," he said slamming down an ace.

No other bright ideas were offered, and there was no stampede of eager helpers rushing to the door. All were understandably and forgivably intent upon their games on this sad, bad Good Friday. The only murmurs from the card players seemed to be 'no bid' or 'pass'. The dice rattling on the tric-trac boards seemed to be tapping out another message; 'We'll not be tricked or tracked away.' But just as John was turning back to the door, Andreas appeared beside him with a friend.

"Cheer up!" said Andreas. "We'll come with you."

His friend looked less than enthusiastic, but nodded as he clutched the collar of his raincoat.

'The better the Day the better the Deed' they say in Scotland. But surely on this occasion it should be, 'The worse the day the greater the deed.'

"God bless you both," said John. "Let's run. We haven't got much time."

They scrambled up the street in blinding rain. Andreas and his friend went off to fetch their spades. John glimpsing a small red-coated figure in the distance, ran to join her. She was standing raptly gazing at the river, holding up her parasol like a tattered banner, and as he came nearer he noticed that her lips were moving.

"Were you singing?" he asked as he reached her side.

"Yes."

"God help us, there's not much to sing about. What was it?"

"Britannia Rule the Waves. I thought it rather apt," said Vivian with a little smile as she tried to light a very wet cigarette.

"Well the waves aren't listening. Let's get on with our barricade. It needs much more support."

As they were gathering rocks to pile against it, Andreas came running with his spade to dig a channel on the farther side of the dip and help divert the water from the gate. His friend appeared a little later, but without a spade.

"Never mind!" said John "You've got two hands and we need them urgently. Just bring us rocks."

The man looked at the water swirling in the dip where most of the rocks were lying. He shook his head and shrugged.

"I'd need gumboots," he said.

"Take mine!" said John.

He tried them on then took them off. "Too big," he sighed with evident relief as he departed. Andreas, digging with all his strength and skill was making little progress. The rising torrent blocked his channel with rocks and mud as fast as he could clear it. The rain poured down. The river roared. Water was spilling over the brim of the dip and lapping at the barricade. The inevitable was about to happen.

Andreas leaned exhausted on his spade. John and Vivian stood helpless by the gate. At that very moment, beneath the sullen roar of water, they heard a thunderous rumbling sound, and watched with disbelief as the path some twenty yards beyond the gate suddenly collapsed across its whole width beneath the pounding river, leaving a wide deep gap which was now deflecting all the water away from the dip in a plunging waterfall to join the thrashing stream much higher up. The gate with its flimsy barricade was no longer under threat.

Andreas shouted, laughed and waved his spade. They all ran up to the gap and looked down at the side exposed to them. Except for a few embedded limestone rocks, nothing showed but clay, which even as they watched was being leached away.

"Thank God for the humble clay. It saved the house," said John. Vivian was not so jubilant. She was gazing with less enchantment at the wildly tumbling scene. The water was now all concentrated below the cliff, on top of which and close to the edge stood her studio.

"If there's clay beneath the path, there'll be clay beneath the cliff," she said.

They ran back to the gate, kicked away the barricade, hurried to the cliff-top wall beside the studio and looked over. In the racing turbulence below they saw great chunks of clay and rock which had fallen from the cliff beneath Charalambos's still-standing garden wall. The cliff face which had been thickly clothed with convolvulus and natural shrubs, was now a sheer bald precipice. They turned to look at the studio immediately beside them.

There are moments in the lives of everyone which remain indelibly imprinted on the mind, haunting by day and intruding in dreams at night. This was such a moment. The outer foundations of the studio had been undermined and were projecting over a yawning cave beneath, gouged out of a deep and unsuspected seam of clay behind the solid-seeming cliff-face. If the rain continued and the spate rose further, the studio might be toppled over and with it all Vivian's aspirations.

There was nothing to be done but hope and pray that the storm might soon expend itself.

"Let's go back to the house and have a glass of wine," said Vivian, grey-faced but still undaunted.

They went back, put on dry clothes, lit a fire, fetched a flask of wine and some Easter eggs and cakes which kind neighbours had brought in. Thus fortified, they sat beside the fire with their unspoken hopes and fears, and listened to the rain.

After an hour or so the noise outside seemed slowly to be lessening.

"Perhaps it's just the wine," said Vivian "but I think it may be clearing up."

John went to the door to look for signs. The sky was brighter, the clouds were thinning, the rain was slackening and the spate was beginning to subside.

"Good news," said John "the depression is moving away. All the water will soon be in the sea, and not a drop came through the roof. The house is intact and the garden will probably recover. Let's have another glass of wine and face the bad news."

"Yes. The studio. What can we do to make it safe again?"

"We're going to build a very solid wall up from the stream bed to secure the exposed foundations and protect the cliff from any further floods."

It was literally a tall order. The height of the cliff was some fifty feet. The wall must be as high and enduringly protective. Only a much experienced mason familiar with the local problems of building among clay and rock, could be trusted with such a formidable task. Who was it to be?

"Andreas, of course," said Vivian.

"Agreed, of course," said John.

Andreas was very busy repairing village houses damaged by the storm. While waiting for him to be freed, John and Vivian settled to their usual work. The storm and its aftermath demanded exorcism.

'Emotion recollected in tranquillity'? For Vivian it was. She painted in bright colours enriched with gold, banners to celebrate the passing of the storm. John still haunted by the sounds of unrelenting rain and plunging water, was less tranquil as he struggled with a dark-keyed song, *molto agitato e espresso.*

One morning after many months, Andreas arrived with a truck-load of rocks, cement, iron rods and a concrete mixer. Then with a shovel, a ladder, a plumb line and a spirit level, and without any other help, he went to work, jauntily, unhurriedly and with never a doubt of his ability. As the wall went up and reached the top, the studio foundations were embedded and massively supported. It was a fortress wall that no future rain or spate would ever threaten.

In peaceful times undisturbed by wars, the sudden threat of destruction to your house, is perhaps as close as most would care to come to grievous loss. But a house may be rebuilt. There is no replacement for the loss of old loved friends who die.

The Muchtar had been very active while the village was filling with people eager to buy land and houses. His work and responsibilities as general arbiter had much increased. He often acted as an independent agent, and in this capacity he could never resist a challenge or a bargain favourable to anyone on whose behalf he might be negotiating, relishing all opposition and argument however heated and prolonged till he had won his point, as of course he always did. All this had taken its toll and he had noticeably aged. Those close to him urged him to relax and delegate. To no avail. "I'm not afraid to die," he would growl with flashing eyes.

Late one afternoon as he was walking up a hill to show a piece of land to some prospective buyers, he stopped for a moment in mid-stride to regain his breath. He then fell dead.

In the evening while the bell was tolling, Andreas came to Irini with the devastating news. No one could believe it. How could that great life-force ever be defeated? The whole village, hushed and stunned, listened unbelieving to the tolling, tolling of the bell.

The news spread quickly beyond Bellapais. Next afternoon, the square was packed with villagers and many others from afar, who had come to pay their last respects. As the flower-decked coffin was carried from the house to the abbey church, everyone rose and stood silent, then fell in behind the grieving family. The open coffin was placed in the centre of the nave and surrounded by the thronging congregation holding lighted candles as the priest led the simple chanting service. When it ended, prominent members of the congregation stepped forward to speak in tribute to Athanasis Athanasiades, the stern but all-understanding Muchtar whose strong and pervasive influence had preserved the gentle 'pais' of Bellapais for some forty years. He would be long remembered and never forgotten by the young as father of the village.

The coffin was carried along narrow tree-lined paths to the little graveyard standing on a small round hill about half a mile away, hedged by banks of sorrel and thicketed by huge tall cypresses.

There the earth was heaped upon the grave among the many grassy mounds.

Each winter took away one or two of the old folks. When they died at a great age, long after their allotted span, their deaths were lightly and naturally accepted by the villagers. They had just 'fallen into the ground' they would say. Many were blessed with long and active lives. As they quietly disappeared, their presences remained - Poumpa's long-lived mother sitting with her bobbin at her accustomed corner in the square, patiently untangling the spinning thread, and dreaming of the thread of life which had sustained her for a century. Frangos who had survived to a ripe old age, was ever to be remembered, stumping up the hill each evening with two cows in tow behind him to be watered at the spring, before he sat wearily on his doorstep and called for a stoup of wine to refresh him while he kicked off his heavy knee-boots.

There were others of tender memory. The old couple opposite Irini who had sat so long and patiently waiting for their deaths were carried away in small black coffins, first one and then, within a month, the other. But their remembered presences still inhabit the garden overgrown with weeds among the jasmine, and the crumbling house, each spring invaded by scores of nesting swallows. Poumpa and Bashi with lesser expectations of long life, had died before their time, leaving a large emptiness which would not be filled.

There was to be another sad untimely death. Costas Kollis was struck down by a mortal illness. He had retired as custodian of the abbey, but was not old by village standards. After some weeks in hospital, convinced that he had not long to live, he asked to be taken back to his beloved village. There surrounded by his family he died. Hosts of villagers and friends flocked to the service in the abbey he had tended and defended with fierce devotion for more than forty years. As an inseparable part of the abbey and a lively convivial friend to villagers and strangers, he had himself become an institution. An irreplaceable part of the spirit of the village died with him.

The deaths of the Muchtar and Costas Kollis heralded the end of a long and happy chapter in the natural life of the village. Despite the scars left by swarming tourists and the unwelcome changes they had brought to simple lives, there had been much stability and preservation of old village ways under the ever watchful eyes of those two guardians.

The Muchtar had died a few months after the April storm of 1971, Costas Kollis in the midst of another storm as unpredictable, and so violent that not just the little village but the whole fabric of the island was to be torn apart.

The storm about to break upon the island was precipitated by deeply divisive disagreements between the two communities. In the summer of 1974 they erupted to a crisis unacceptable to the Turks who reacted swiftly. The island was suddenly at war within itself.

One morning a village friend leaned over the gate and said, "There's been a coup." John and Vivian had listened to the early morning programme over the radio, and vaguely puzzled had heard nothing but martial music instead of the usual news. They listened again. There had indeed been a coup. The Government had been overthrown. A twenty four hour curfew had been imposed throughout the island. Anyone appearing in the streets would be shot. That was the news. Brief and bleak.

During the next five days there were further bulletins, though the situation remained confused and unpredictable. Despite the continuing curfew, women needing food for their families went out to the village shops which remained open till they were emptied. Ulla Boola came undaunted in the mornings, and Andreas jaunty as ever to do some gardening, but the prevailing mood among the villagers was far from sanguine as they whispered rumours of a retaliatory invasion from the Turkish mainland only forty miles away across the sea.

The local body of the National Guard was gathering in the hills. Short bursts of gun-fire ripped the air as they prepared their weapons and defences. The whole village was alert and tense as it waited, scanning the sea for an approaching fleet.

On the sixth day after the coup the fleet arrived as announced over the radio. A Turkish force had invaded the island at dawn, the main assault directed along the coast some four or five miles below and beyond the village. Not that anyone needed to be told. At five o'clock the villagers had been startled from their beds by the noise of distant gun-fire and loud return fire from the hills. As they looked out from their roof-tops they saw ships already close in-shore and more approaching, and heard the crumps of bombs from escorting planes flying in the distance along the shore.

The village was soon astir, cocks crowing in alarm, dogs barking, donkeys braying their old sad lament, the usually sleepy breakfast chatter in nearby houses loud and strident. Men gathered in the square to debate, agree or disagree about what they should or could do. Women and children from the lower part of the village, hurried through the streets seeking the shelter of less vulnerable houses in the lee of the hill above Irini. Ulla Boola, reluctantly among them, came to ask for a pot of tea to comfort them. Scant comfort, but enough to revive their resilient spirits as they huddled in empty houses beneath the steep protection of the hill.

Though the village was not yet directly under threat, there was during those first few hours, one most inconvenient casualty. The electricity was suddenly cut off. It was an extremely hot July. Midday temperatures were hovering around 104 degrees Fahrenheit. There were now no cooling fans. Refrigerators soon became hot boxes full of rotting food. Vivian sweated in the kitchen for the next few days rescuing and cooking what could be salvaged, baking Melba toast from mouldering loaves of bread.

On the following day as the close and distant gun-fire continued, fighter planes and scores of helicopters appeared high overhead, flying south to inland targets. Beyond the range of the guns positioned in the hills, they flew unscathed, squadron after squadron in undisturbed formation. Though the signs were obvious enough that sooner or later the village would be invaded, it seemed to be the only haven for those fleeing from their own bombarded coastal villages. They came swarming, desperately seeking accommodation. Unoccupied rooms and houses were opened to them for the few remaining days before the village was to be captured. Just in time, before that happened, most of them and a number of their host villagers with their families were able to escape across the hills.

The British Bases in the southern part of the island were broadcasting information and advice to civilians. Some thousands had already been evacuated by road convoy from Nicosia to the safety of the Sovereign Bases. As soon as could be arranged, British Navy ships would be sent to the northern shore to take aboard all residents and tourists there who wished to leave. Those who chose to stay behind were advised to keep strictly to their houses. John and Vivian whose natural habits confined them to the house, continued with their usual occupations, Vivian starting a new picture, John finishing a song.

In the evening they went down to the square to talk with friends. The air was electric with alarm, and the noise of low flying aircraft crackling overhead. Voices were raised in anger or dismay. Young men, stubbornly defiant, stood among others wide-eyed in disbelief. Exhausted refugees still arriving, were arguing with little hope their chances of survival. A group of National Guardsmen passed by, grim and silent after a long day in the hills. A few old men sat at their accustomed tables, shrugging and shaking their heads. Only Dimitri ambling to and fro carrying coffee at his own slow unhurried pace, remained patient and equable as ever, the last reminder it seemed, of the peaceful village already in disruption. What would the next day bring?

At first an unexpected silence. A cock crowed announcing sunrise, shook its wings and then perhaps reassured fell silent. No other sound disturbed the stillness. The auguries were hopeful. The early morning radio news was promising. A cease-fire had been arranged for four o'clock that afternoon. Vivian went to tell the women crowded with their fretting children in the nearby houses. They were not impressed. While they were talking the gun-fire started again, and no one was to be convinced that it was going to stop at four in the afternoon. (It didn't). Two of the women were plucking a stray hen they had caught and killed for the pot. They had some bread and other scraps of food they'd snatched up and brought with them, and would stay where they were in safety with their children, till the news could be believed.

A little later, though still early, two close friends appeared at the gate and with them their young daughter and their little house-maid. Their house high on the hill above the village was directly in the line of fire between the attack and the defence, and was likely soon to become untenable. Irini was much less exposed. Could they stay for a day or two? Of course. They could sleep in the erstwhile guest house. There were only two beds but a couple of mattresses could be put on the floor for the young ones. They'd need no blankets in the oppressive heat. In the day-time they could be in Irini, watching through the windows the developing scene below, and discussing together what the prospects seemed to hold.

More ships were arriving and more planes opposed by anti-aircraft fire. The invaders and defenders must by now be heavily engaged along the coast. Though it was impossible to judge at a distance of four or five miles how the battle might be swaying, whether or not a bridgehead had been established, there could be little doubt that the situation was critical. Towards the middle of the morning all eyes turned suddenly from the frontal scene to the hills behind the village where a forest fire was raging. One spark from a bullet striking stone would be enough to set alight the grass dried to tinder in the withering heat of that July. Smoke billowed from the flames which were soon engulfing trees. A hot wind sprang up, blowing cinders and fine ash to fill the already stifling air and settle like a grey mantle on the garden. After some hours of tense anxiety, the fire abated and burned itself out before it reached the village. But it had been a most unwelcome interlude in the prevailing situation.

The 'cease-fire' hour of four o'clock came and passed unheeded. To acutely listening ears, the distant gunfire seemed to be drawing closer. Perhaps some troops had landed and were advancing though none were to be seen. Later in the afternoon, Vivian running to her studio along the path beneath the vines, was halted not only by the usual buzzing hornets. Bullets were whizzing through the vine leaves. From which direction they were coming she didn't linger to investigate, prudently withdrawing to the protection of Irini.

In the evening as the light began to fade, though not the now less distant sounds of battle, they all sat down to supper in the patio. Vivian had saved a chicken from the refrigerator and prepared a curry. They ate by candle light, and their talk though earnest was subdued. Both were suddenly forbidden. A National Guardsman watching and listening at his post nearby, signalled that the light must be doused and the talk must stop. The meal continued under starlight; Cassiopeia, the Plough and the Little Dipper. What did they foretell? The talk was reduced to whispered speculations and murmured toasts as they raised their glasses to each other, and to the stars. As they groped their way in darkness to their beds, they wondered with some foreboding what they might awake to in the morning. It was to be a crucial day for all of them.

Quite unexpectedly they woke again to silence. John and Vivian got up with the sun and found their friends dressed and ready to depart at once. They had decided to take advantage of the lull, unlikely to last for long, and drive across the hills to Nicosia. Unidentified as Greeks they might (and did) come under fire from the hill defences, but as Greeks they were, that was a risk they had to take if they were to escape capture by the invaders. They had a powerful car and would avoid main roads by keeping to little used by-ways well known to them. It was now or never. Had they lingered for another day they would surely have been trapped. In the event they reached Nicosia unchallenged and unharmed.

Soon after they had left the exchange of fire resumed. It was louder and closer and the sounds had changed to the crack and rattle of rifles and machine-guns, and more ominously the heavy thud of mortar shells. If one of those came through the roof there would be not much left of anyone upstairs. John and Vivian went down to the kitchen, and listened to the news. The invaders were ashore and evidently advancing. The British Bases radio was announcing that two Navy frigates and the aircraft carrier HMS Hermes were standing off the coast ready to take on board all civilians of whatever nationality who chose to leave. Many hundreds were expected. They were instructed to gather at designated assembly points along the shore. Helicopters would ferry them to the ships which would take them to the Sovereign Bases. Haste was urged.

John and Vivian reviewed the situation. Neither of them had any wish to leave, but it seemed only sensible to discuss the pros and cons. Vivian was stubbornly for staying. Irini was where they belonged, surrounded by all their treasured possessions, books, pictures, stacks of canvasses in the studio waiting to be painted, music manuscripts and tape records of

John's songs, the great piano and much else. If they left, the house might be commandeered or looted by the soldiers who would soon be in the village. But her chief impulse for remaining sprang from curiosity and the challenge of coming events. There was plenty of canned food in the larder and water in the tanks. They would survive and face a new adventure. John was not so sure. His chief thought was for Vivian. No one could tell what might lie ahead when the village was overrun by troops. Vivian might be caught by a bullet, or if he himself were, she might be left without support. Life and limb were more immediate considerations than possessions. Why not go to the Bases for a week and then return when the situation had cooled and settled down a bit?

They argued for about an hour, ducking under the kitchen table now and then when the mortar fire came uncomfortably close. Though they reached no complete agreement, they decided that they would stay.

"A committee of two never comes to a unanimous conclusion," said Vivian. "As usual we really need a casting vote."

The end of their disputation coincided with some abatement of the mortar fire. Vivian set about preparing lunch. John went upstairs to finish writing down a song, appropriately enough a setting of a Border Ballad about a day of battle. 'Bonnie George Campbell rode out on a day... Hame cam his guid horse, but never cam he...'

An hour or so later he heard voices in the kitchen and went down to investigate. A tall young British corporal from the United Nations unit in the island, was talking with some urgency to Vivian He had come to offer them, among others in the village, safe passage to HMS Hermes. An escort of two Bren Gun carriers was waiting at the gate.

"It's very kind of you," said John, "but we've both decided we should stay."

"Well I think you ought to change your minds."

"Why?"

"Judging from what I've seen in Kyrenia, most certainly you should. It's a pretty grisly sight. And my orders are to advise you urgently to come."

John and Vivian looked at each other for a long searching moment, Vivian giving no hint of what was in her mind, John committed to the casting vote. The corporal frowned and glanced impatiently at his watch.

"The troops are already nearly at the bottom of the hill," he said.

"How long have we to decide?" John asked.

"Two minutes. Hermes will be sailing in about an hour."

John looked at Vivian again and sighed.

"OK we'll come," he said, not ungraciously he hoped.

It took a little longer than two minutes to throw some clothes into a suitcase, find passports and some money, lock the house and leave.

A score or so of tourists and some others were waiting in the square beside their cars. As the corporal was giving them instructions, "Keep close and don't stop." Vivian pleaded with him to stop just once when they passed Doc Fraser's house so that he could join them should he be there.

"If he's outside and ready," said the corporal, "we'll pick him up. If not we must press on. We're running late."

An elderly villager came up and asked if there was room in the car for his wife, himself and his small daughter.

"Plenty," said John, "the back seat's empty, but you may not be safe if the cars are searched for Greeks."

"We'll take that risk," said the old man as they all climbed in.

Though most of the refugees and some of the villagers had vanished, the square was filled with many who couldn't or wouldn't leave. Those who couldn't shrugged and said "If we could we would. *Sto kalo.*" Those who wouldn't, smiled and waved. "Come back soon," they said.

"We'll be back within a week," said John.

The convoy moved away, one Bren Gun carrier in the lead, blue flags fluttering, the other closely in the rear. As they came to the Doc's house they slowed while John and Vivian looked out for that unmistakable small figure, John with his hand on the horn. There was no sign of him. Perhaps he had already left? (He hadn't. They later learned that he was watching un-seen inside the house as the convoy paused, having decided to stay with the villagers. For that decision, and the support and help he gave them, he was to become a legend in the village).

At the bottom of the hill they met the Turkish troops advancing from Kyrenia three miles behind them and turning at the cross roads for the last steep mile to Bellapais. The leading officer waved the convoy past unchallenged, though it had yet to run the gauntlet of the troops armed with rifles, machine-guns or bazookas at the ready, marching in a column three miles long on both sides of the road. Their eyes were deeply sunken, their faces burned dark by the blazing sun. Some seemed to be near the limit of exhaustion, but all were obviously formidable and well disciplined. On and on they marched in silence, staring straight ahead as in a dream, with not even a glance at the blue-flagged Bren Gun carriers. They were wearily intent only upon their next objective.

Bellapais was to be occupied, though not with violence. No villagers were injured. The abbey and the houses were not damaged. The Tree of Idleness and Dimitri's coffee shop remained freely open. But the villagers were to suffer much alarm and shock under the immediate severities of military occupation. Men of fighting age were taken prisoner and deported, not to be released for many months. The women and all other remaining villagers were confined to the village under curfew. The shops were empty, and there was no possible access to the usual markets in Kyrenia or Nicosia. How then could the villagers be fed? The United Nations came swiftly to the rescue, bringing quantities of food, truckloads of gas to cook it and many other subsidiary household needs. No one was to starve and none went even hungry.

Later the military restrictions would be considerably relaxed, and the villagers gradually recovering their spirits settled down to make the best of the situation, at least for a year or so. Kyrenia on the contrary had been an essential military objective to be taken at any cost. As the convoy reached it and drove slowly through the streets, the scars and debris of destructive battle were everywhere to be seen, the sounds of distant gunfire heard in Bellapais now translated into the immediate reality of sights, grim and stark. The little town was empty and forlorn. Smashed and crumpled cars, and here and there a derelict tank, lay about where they had been crippled and abandoned. The familiar shops and office buildings, riddled with bullet holes were scarcely recognizable, their windows staring black and empty, the shattered glass littering the pavements. The smell of death was in the air. A sprawling corpse was glimpsed in the garden of a little house. Homeless dogs snarled and fought for scraps of rotting food among stinking garbage bins.

The convoy, weaving through the deserted but obstructed streets came to its destination outside the old Dome Hotel on the seafront. Beside it there was a large car park, kept empty for the helicopters landing and taking off with passengers to HMS Hermes lying a mile or so offshore.

"Over to you now," said the corporal as John thanked him for his patience and safe passage. "Just obeying orders," he replied with a weary smile. "You're a bit obstinate, but so am I, and I got you here in time. All you have to do is get aboard. No problem. Bon voyage."

There was however one small immediate problem. Where to leave the car? Every nearby street was crammed with hastily abandoned cars. Many were large and some quite new. There was little chance it seemed that these would ever be recovered by their owners. But perhaps a small old Morris Minor might not be noticed among such a rich array. John tucked it into a little nook beside the parking place. "It's hardly a coveted prize of war," he murmured as he locked it and pocketed the key, "but I wonder if we'll ever see it again."

They joined the last few groups waiting for the helicopters. Among them there were old people who had been forced to abandon their houses so suddenly and unexpectedly that they had had no time to pack, and scarcely time to dress. One or two were even without shoes. There were also many tourists, caught on the beaches without access to essential possessions, passports, money, clothes. Young women stood barefoot and empty-handed in their bikinis. The great ship took them all, and late in the afternoon set course, stopping during the night along the coast to take more aboard. Early next morning all were put ashore at Akrotiri, the RAF component of the British Bases where John and Vivian were expecting to stay for a week before their return to Bellapais.

Hermes had brought them swiftly and smoothly, and as the helicopter put them gently down, it occurred to them that the overland journey back was likely to be neither swift nor smooth. They could drive by bus or taxi across the Greek-held south to the frontier wherever that might be. What then? By persuasion and a show of passports they might get through. If so, for the rest of the way they would have to rely on passing transport to take them to Kyrenia, and find the car perhaps. Both unlikely. It could hardly be called a plan, but such were their vague intentions, based on hope and luck.

They were quickly to be disillusioned. The RAF station, busily active at the best of times, and now alert for any emergencies, was already embarrassed with hundreds of evacuees. No more could possibly be fed or even accommodated. Every extra bed was filled.

"Well here we are, stranded far from home," said Vivian. "We can't get back to the village on our feet, and there's not a taxi or a bus in sight. Where do we go now?"

The answer came not from the equally rueful John, but from a trim and cheerful air hostess who announced that two large RAF transport planes were waiting on the runway, ready to fly all British subjects back to England. A most handsome gesture, offering them the only way out of their predicament, though all against their ill-planned intentions. There was no alternative.

That evening they found themselves in London. They stayed with friends and made the most of an unexpected holiday, but the village, now some 3,000 miles away was ever present in their minds and in the news. In the daily papers they read that the invasion was advancing to occupy much territory in the northern sector of the island, and that in its wake houses were being looted. The BBC news bulletins upon the general situation were far from optimistic. Television commentaries and scenes were closely following events. One programme showed Bellapais, and their fellow villagers queueing for food rations in the Tree of Idleness, Doc Fraser in their midst cheerfully scurrying about. They longed to get back to the village, join the indefatigable Doc, do everything they could to help the villagers, and also in their own interests be there to protect the house.

There was no immediate possibility of returning. The island was in chaos. Communications were disrupted. The International airport in Nicosia was closed. Sea passages to the southern ports were few, and re-entry to the island at that time was forbidden. Eventually they flew to Athens, joined a boat to Limassol and from there in accordance with their original plan, drove by taxi to the frontier now established at the edge of Nicosia. After close scrutiny of their passports at the check-point bristling with guns among the sandbags, they were taken by Turkish convoy to sad Kyrenia and thence to Bellapais, wondering as they drove up through the bare, burned hills what they might expect after not a week, but more than two months absence.

The square was swarming with strangers, middle-aged and older men, sitting listlessly in the pale sunshine or pacing aimlessly round the little central garden, wrapped in brooding silence, their faces white and blank. They were refugees, some from deserted coastal villages and many from Kyrenia, shopkeepers, tradesmen and artisans some of whom John and Vivian knew and talked with. Their stories were all the same. In their flight they had lost everything except the clothes they stood in. Shops, the tools of their trades and with them their livelihoods and future hopes. There was little that could be said in truth to offer any comfort, except that they would surely find their lives again. They just shook their heads and shrugged.

Among them there was one undaunted spirit, Yannis Cleanthos, stocky, strong and irrepressible, an old friend, and until captured, Curator of Kyrenia Castle. He came up with an outstretched hand and a beaming smile. "Welcome back!" he said, "Come and have a glass of wine and let's swap our news."

They went into the Tree of Idleness where Sawas Kortellis the imperturbable proprietor was surveying his still ample stock of wine behind the bar. Tall and somewhat reserved, his usually impassive face relaxed in a quiet smile, though lately there had been little enough to smile about. He and Yannis had just been released from imprisonment, and the memory was vivid though they made light of it now that they were free. John and Vivian soon disposed of their small news and were impatient to hear about the local situation.

The village was quiet and had returned to some semblance of normality. The curfew had been lifted during the hours of daylight, so everyone could go about and meet without restriction until dusk. The women were being regularly supplied by the United Nations with their household needs, and their men were gradually being released to them. The refugees had been taken in to spare rooms and empty houses, and none went hungry. The villagers had few complaints. They were being treated very well.

"But where are all the soldiers?" Vivian asked in some puzzlement.

The occupying garrison had been withdrawn to a camp outside the village, leaving a sergeant of Police (Sergeant Khalil) to keep order in the village. Happily he was a patient understanding man who had been readily accepted by the villagers.

"While we were in London we read and heard reports of looting. Has there been any here?" John asked.

Well of course there had been. After all, that was to be expected of fighting troops everywhere. Houses left unoccupied were especially vulnerable.

"I think it's time we went to see what ours looks like," said Vivian.

As they walked up to the house, they braced themselves against expected shocks. What would they find? Empty drawers and cupboards, floors littered with books and clothes in the search for hidden cash or anything readily saleable? The visions multiplied with every step till they reached the house.

It looked the same as ever. No broken windows or other signs of forced entry met their first swift glances. As they went through the gate, the back door suddenly opened, and there outside it to their astonishment stood Ulla Boola. They rushed to her with bone-crushing hugs and bombarded her with questions. How was she? Very well she said, and looked it. How had she got into the house? She had her own set of keys. Didn't they remember? How long had she been in it? Since the day after they had left. Her husband and her son had been taken prisoner, so she had locked her own house and moved in with her strapping daughter, to watch over it and keep the garden alive. The beds were very comfortable, she added with a contented smile. Had she been disturbed by anyone trying to get into the house and take it over? No, she hadn't. Later they learned that on more than one occasion she had been. Intruders had come banging on the door, demanding entry and occupation. They had got no further and had soon fled at the sight of her mighty figure. She had never left the house unguarded. How then had she managed for food? Her daughter had collected their U.N. rations and they had eaten well.

Among many more, there was one last baffling question which was never solved. There were no communications between the two sides of the island at that time, yet somehow Ulla Boola had got wind of their return, God alone knows how, and was expecting them.

"Ella mesa," *Come inside,* she said. "Elpiso alla ine indaxi." *I hope you'll find everything all right.*

The kitchen was scrubbed and clean, all the dishes, plates and cooking pans immaculate in their places. And in the refrigerator (the electricity having been long restored) there was ice and food and wine awaiting them. Upstairs everything was exactly as it had been left, not a chair, a table or a book out of place. The beds had been freshly made, and in a drawer, safely tucked away, John found £20 in English notes he had inadvertently left on the dressing table in the haste of packing.

Outside, the paths were newly swept, the garden was tidy, watered and weeded, and looking a great deal better than when they last had seen it, wilting in the summer heat and strewn with ashes from the forest fire. The indomitable Ulla Boola stood there beaming happily. But for her, the house would very likely have been the wreck John and Vivian had imagined as they had walked up from the square. As they hugged her again and tried to thank her, she just shrugged and said "Tipote" *It is nothing.* She had expected nothing in return, and when her large warm hand was filled with something more tangible than words, she accepted it only after prolonged insistence. The saving of the house had been wholly and alone by great, beloved Ulla Boola, uninfluenced by luck or chance. Now only by unexpected luck and chance against all odds could they hope to find the car.

Next day they went down to Kyrenia to look for it with little hope. At best they might perhaps pass it in the street, driven by a new owner. More likely it would just have disappeared. But as they came to the Dome Hotel to look first where they had left it, there to their sudden disbelief it stood, alone, still locked, untouched, unscratched. The explanation soon became apparent. By great good luck one tyre was flat. Who would have been bothered to pick a small locked car with one flat tyre when there had been so many others to choose, large and ready to drive away? By further chance the battery was also flat, but their luck still held. They found a mechanic who changed the tyre and repaired the battery, topped up the radiator which was almost dry, filled the petrol tank, and after further checks pronounced the little car as good as new. John and Vivian then drove up to Bellapais to start their lives afresh, and find out what they could do for the villagers and the refugees.

A great deal was already being done, not only by the United Nations. The Red Cross, hard-pressed by other villages in need, was sending clothes and whatever else could be spared from limited supplies. A clinic had been opened in the old school house, attended by Turkish army medical officers and Doc Fraser, assisted by village girls, chief among them, Panzelitza as quick and conscientious as had been her father Costas Kollis. Thus in the midst of war a service was being provided which the village had never known in all its peaceful years. Doc Fraser worked happily with the Turkish doctors in the clinic, and on his own initiative used it further to give protective inoculation to all the village children. His thought was only for the villagers as he bounded from house to house, or stood puffing at his pipe to talk and laugh with anyone seeking his advice and help. His spirit was infectious. Exuding cheerfulness and confidence, he was already a living legend in the village.

A new Muchtar, Sotiris Pheneris, a very determined, practical and thoughtful young man in his early thirties, had been appointed to manage the daily affairs in the village and tackle the various problems which remained, not the least of which was re-housing refugees as the village men returned to houses already overfilled. He had formed a committee and with their help and the good will of the villagers had made good progress.

John and Vivian went to see him in his house.

"You seem to have everything organized," said John, "but surely there must be something useful left for us to do?"

"Well, not everything is organized. We've somehow managed to find extra room for the refugees. All at least have beds. But we have to think of the winter, only a few months away. We're very short of blankets as the villagers have had to share theirs with the refugees. We need warm clothes for everyone and new shoes for the children which we've been unable to buy as we usually do at this time of the year."

"Tell us what you need and we'll make it our job to get it."

A few days later Sotiris produced a long list of clothes and shoes of all sizes for the children, but blankets were the most immediate need. John and Vivian were able to pass the message to friends in touch with the Red Cross on the other side of the island. Less than a week later two truck-loads of blankets arrived to be distributed in the square.

It would be some months before the clothes and shoes arrived in quantity, but in the meanwhile a small beginning could be made. James Pickering had returned to the village for a fleeting visit, eager to offer help which included all the clothes in his house. John and Vivian searched their cupboards for winter shirts and dresses, cardigans and jackets. Ulla Boola cheerfully accepted one of John's jerseys not quite big enough for her, and Andreas a tweed jacket much too large. The rest were handed over to the Muchtar for the neediest.

That was just a trickle. An idea occurred to Vivian which was to swell it to a flood. There were many old friends in the UK, the USA and elsewhere who had known and loved the village. Surely they would respond to an appeal? She wrote letters by the score asking them to collect and send warm clothes, old or new, or cheques in lieu to buy them locally when possible. All to be sent to the Red Cross in Nicosia who would get them through to the village. The response beyond all hopeful expectations, was immediate and imaginative. One friend after rifling her own cupboards, canvassed all the houses in her street for further contributions. Another persuaded a Cyprus Tourist agency in London to accept all parcels and have them sent out, free of charge by air freight. Another, working as a doctor far away in Muscat, appealed to the Save the Children Fund there. They held a jumble sale and with the proceeds went to the bazaar and bought scores of children's shoes (all new and made in Cyprus!), then persuaded the RAF stationed there to fly them to the island. Yet another friend in the north of England spent two months collecting new clothes from factories, and then wrote to announce that two tons of them were packed and ready to be shipped out. There were many smaller parcels and also cheques, some very handsome.

At the end of three months Sotiris called a stop. Everyone was by then well clothed and shod. It had been a spontaneously generous tribute to the village by those who remembered it with love. There was a small and happy coda to be added. Some months later as spring approached, the *Kopelles* of the village came to Vivian with a list of their names and measurements, asking her to write to the Red Cross for frocks to be made and sent to them in for Easter. The list was sent and a few weeks later all the frocks arrived, sizes, designs and colours as requested. The girls strolled happily together in the square on Easter Day, dressed in their bright new frocks, innocently unaware that it was to be the last but one that they would see in Bellapais.

The winter passed well enough. The last of the men were back and united with their families. Old friends among the co-villagers who had been away during the invasion were returning, some to stay, and with them a few newcomers to take occupation of houses bought before the troubles had erupted. Other friends, especially Robert Crawford the American Ambassador, his wife and members of his staff, came often to brighten the weekends.

Sotiris and his committee had solved their most pressing problems. The refugees and the villagers slept warm beneath their blankets. Despite a scarcity of teachers and new books, the school had been re-opened and the children seemed quite happy as they ran in the playground playing the old game lately learned, of 'chase and capture'.

Sergeant Khalil had become a familiar figure. Benign and helpful, he sat in his office above the old school house in the mornings, ready to answer any question or complaint. Later he strolled or sat with the villagers in the square. At first he had been armed with a rifle slung across his shoulder, but soon discarded it. He had the authority and also the trust of the villagers without it, and had been accepted with understanding and even affection for himself in the discharge of his necessary duties. Of course the troops in their nearby camp were alert to come to his support if ever needed. Though they never were, they showed their presence and their strength in case anyone might doubt it. Each day, early in the morning they took their exercise running with pounding feet along the paths, in, around and above the village, stripped to the waist and singing in full throated response to their leader. It was a disturbing awakening, perhaps even for the soldiers. Once as they passed the gate, a straggler in the rear dropped off for a rest, and came panting into the studio where Vivian was already at work.

"Me very strong!" he declared by way of introduction, flexing his arms but wilting at the knees.

"Me too." said Vivian, flourishing a paint brush.

These were only small disturbances. The village was otherwise quiet, and the villagers almost all deprived of their usual work, occupied their empty days as best they could. Towards the end of the year the village became quieter still and emptier, as the refugees began to drift away, crossing to the other side of the island to find work and pick up the threads of their lives again, leaving houses now unoccupied by villagers who had escaped and would not return, and empty chairs and tables in the square. The remaining villagers drew more closely together, especially at festive times.

After the turn of the year as Easter was approaching, the old spirit of the village came to life again. On Green Monday men and women gathered at midday in the Tree of Idleness, bringing green vegetables from their gardens, salads, cakes and wine. Everyone was welcome including Sergeant Khalil as though one of the family. It was a day of hope and laughter. All that sunny afternoon there was music and singing. The dancing was led by the irrepressible Yannis whose deep voice rose in song after song and great gusts of laughter as he leapt and slapped his legs in dance after dance till the evening curfew hour. A month later Easter came and though unheralded by the jubilantly swinging abbey bell, brought further celebrations and rising hopes for the future of the village. They were not to be fulfilled for long. No one could foretell the future, though many had forebodings. The village was slowly running down. The shops, though open, had little on their shelves. The Tree of Idleness still had small stocks of food and wine, and in the evenings a few tables would be laid, but there was little custom since nobody was earning any money. The villagers sat about the square in desultory talk and dejected speculation.

Sotiris though relieved of many responsibilities, was concerned with others which had arisen. He had no funds left to pay for the upkeep of the village, and no volunteers were forthcoming to sweep the streets, collect and dispose of garbage and keep the village in good repair. No one was inclined to do such work unpaid.

"What can I do?" asked Sotiris in despair.

"You can tax us for the wages," John suggested.

"No one can afford to pay taxes."

"Well just tax us foreigners. We have our pensions and some money in the bank. It's the only solution."

The streets were cleaned and swept again, and the village, spruce and tidy took a short new lease of life seeming almost to have returned to its immemorial peace as it stirred itself awake for a little while, then slept through the drowsy summer. The sleep was fitfully disturbed by dreams of the looming future. What would it bring?

Autumn came with whispering breezes, bringing rumours of something more in the air than just the change of season. The villagers roused themselves uneasily and looked about for signs which might give substance to the rumours. They soon noticed that the equable and amiable Khalil had lately become somewhat reserved. He seemed worried and unhappy Had he perhaps been instructed to prepare himself to give the villagers bad news? There were other signs, perhaps more sinister, to be interpreted. Sotiris and his committee, summoned one day to Kyrenia for a long interview with the police, had returned to the village, grim and silent. Doc Fraser in his devotion to the villagers, had been driving across the Green line to bring them brandy and cigarettes from the Greek side of Nicosia, since none at that time were available in Kyrenia. On his return one afternoon he had been arrested at the check point. The car was searched and his booty confiscated. The Customs Officer understanding the Doc's altruistic motives, fined him lightly, but told him that he must leave the village and would not be allowed to return.

In the village, rumours and counter-rumours multiplied and spread, supported or dismissed by every real or imagined sign of impending doom. Winter brought the long awaited, harsh and wintry truth.

The whole Greek population of the village was to be evicted to the Greek-held south.

There was no official announcement. The news emerged as just another rumour. But this time it persisted. Sotiris and others had been long resigned to the inevitable fate of the village, and Khalil when pressed could not deny it. The villagers faced a disaster which they were powerless to resist. All their ancestral ties, their deeply rooted love for the village were to be suddenly, incomprehensibly disrupted, their houses, orchards and inherited lands lost forever, their own fates unpredictable.

Their grief was aggravated by the dilemma of their situation. Held captive in the village for more than eighteen months, though well treated by their captors, the men were earning nothing to sustain their careers and their families. A man must work, his wife must have the confidence of security, and the children must be educated beyond the local school. There were no prospects in the village of such hopes. All instincts were fiercely, stubbornly for staying, but how could they prevail against the opposing forces of reality and survival? That was the agony of the dilemma.

As the vines and figs and mulberries were coming into leaf, and the swifts and swallows came flying in, the villagers began to prepare for the fateful exodus. Chickens, hens and cocks, turkeys and rabbits in the gardens were killed and eaten. Trees were plucked of fruit. Mules and donkeys were taken to the hills and there released. Room by room, houses were stripped and emptied. Trucks and lorries came to be logged and piled high with beds and mattresses, blankets and bright patchwork bedspreads, bundles of clothes and shoes and old well-worn knee-boots, chairs and tables and great carved wooden chests, kitchen stoves and cupboards, pots and pans, wine-stained gourds and demijohns. All the impedimenta of houses long lived in, and on top of the precariously balanced loads the most treasured family possessions, framed photographs of weddings, precious trinkets, children's toys and linen lovingly embroidered by generations of daughters laughing and singing as they had sat and stitched beneath a shady tree outside their doors when the village had been in its high summer. Intimate evocations of past joy and settled happiness.

Friends and neighbours watched and helped with the loading, waiting for their own turn. Women wept. Their men stubbornly defiant or wearily resigned, kept their composure and tried to comfort them. The children gazed silent and bewildered, not believing that they would never see their homes again. Early in the mornings the heavily laden trucks and lorries pulled out from the square, taking away dear friends perhaps never again to be seen. As they disappeared down the hill and out of sight, all the joyful innocence of the village slowly vanished with them. They who had welcomed refugees with their gentle generosity were themselves now refugees.

John and Vivian went to bid inarticulate farewells to those they were able to find amidst the confusion of departure.
They found Sotiris about to leave, standing among the debris of his empty house, beside him his despairing wife and three small unruly sons. He had striven hard and long to hold the village together under the threat he had long foreseen. Now accepting the inevitable he stood there, calm and stolid. As he held out his hand in a last brief greeting and farewell, he showed no sign of his defeated hopes. Somewhere, somehow he and his family would survive.

Ulla Boola was sitting in her house when they went to say goodbye to her the evening before she left. She sat wordlessly gazing at the floor, sighing and shrugging her mighty shoulders, her burly husband and their usually lively daughter sitting mutely with her, surrounded by all their possessions packed and ready for the lorry in the morning. There was nothing to be said to relieve the silence of despair. John and Vivian fumbled helplessly for words, all useless with not even a truthful scrap of comfort, for there was none. Ulla Boola had saved Irini for them, and now in her extremity they were powerless to save her own house for her.

As the village emptied, old friends came up to Irini, some with potted plants and flowers for remembrance, bringing to mind

Poumpa and others who had died when the village was in its happy hey-day. Andreas came to sit with them for the last time in the house he had helped to build. He knew every joist and beam, every roof and floor tile, and in the garden every flagstone he had laid for paths and steps and water channels, had built the little guest house and the great protective cliff wall. His imprint would remain upon everything he had touched and undertaken, and beyond that his close and jaunty, never-failing friendship. He was part of the fabric of Irini as of their daily lives. They sat for an hour or two over wine and talk about the good years, delaying the moment of unbelievable finality. When he left they stood at the door long after his familiar footstep had faded in the darkness and the gate clicked shut behind him.

The last to leave was the all-enduring sleepy-eyed Dimitri. He came ambling up the hill at his usual unhurried pace to say goodbye, looking sad and puzzled but unruffled and serene as ever. As they talked they reminded him that he had been the first to greet them in the square nearly a quarter of a century ago. Now, instead of a bottle of cold beer as on that occasion, he had brought a little flask of valetudinary wine which he put into their hands with a gentle smile as he departed.

With Dimitri, the host of Bellapais and the very symbol of its peace and hospitality, went the last vestige of the village as they had known it and the villagers of old.

THE BELL HANGS SILENT

The abbey bell had long been silent. Soon after the occupation of the village, the daily chimes and festive peals had ceased. It was only in the imagination that the bell now tolled for the forsaken village. The silence was complete, all the other familiar sounds of life now also stilled. No cocks crowed in the mornings among their clucking hens, waking the households to the clatter of plates and breakfast chatter. Donkeys no longer clip-clopped on the cobbles taking the men away to work. Outside front doors no spindles squeaked as old women spun their silk and young women laughed and gossiped and called to their children in the gardens. No voices echoed from the square calling "Ella Dimitri!" and on Sunday mornings no quavering plain song came up from the abbey church.

In the evenings no men came riding home after long days in the fields to join their greeting families, put their hungry braying donkeys to the byre, and talk for an hour or two over supper as plates were scraped and glasses clinked in homely harmony, till it was time to sleep and close the creaking shutters.

Not a voice or a footstep stirred the brooding stillness in the empty streets and houses and the deserted square. The village was like a graveyard, so eerie and so total was the stillness and the silence.

All about, on paths and in bare rooms there were the signs of confused departures, and relics abandoned or forgotten in the haste and perplexity of exodus, plates and dishes from a last meal left behind, kitchen taps left open and spouting floods of water. Scattered on floors lay old household remnants, a rickety chair perhaps, a rusty pot, a broken jug, and small forlorn belongings, a woman's shoe, a man's hat, a doll. On the paths, fragments of glasses and other fragile objects dropped and shattered, lay trampled among rubbish and the strewn chips and nails of packing cases.

The desolation was as haunting as the silence.

As the days and weeks crawled by, John and Vivian thought and dreamed about the village in its innocence, as it had been when first they had glimpsed it in the distance, pristine and shining white beneath the sun. Then as now it had been quiet and still, but in those times underneath the soporific silence, the murmur of innumerable small sounds, and the steady pulse of the bell announcing its occasions, had told that the village was abundantly alive.

They dreamt of dreams fulfilled in that once perfect ambience. Their thoughts were crowded with memories of the men and women, young and old, the sturdy 'characters' and the lively children who had made the village what it had been, imprinted by the touch of gentle lives. What did the future hold? Were the houses to be left to crumble slowly into ruin and decay under winter rains and storms, perhaps never to be inhabited again? These sad questions were soon answered by events. The village was to be spared decay and ruin. Life returned.

POSTLUDE

E vacuation soon became widespread. The island was in a state of flux, as Greeks moved from the north to the security of the Greek-held south, and Turks from the south to the protection of the newly occupied north. Whole populations of towns and villages were changing places in hope or desperation.

The villagers of Mari, a small Turkish village in the south were destined for Bellapais. One morning the trucks and lorries reappeared with the first of the new people and their possessions. For many days the streets were choked with traffic and littered with unloaded cargoes. As houses were allotted and the newcomers took in their possessions, the streets were cleared again to make way for the next arrivals. So it went on till the last trucks and lorries sped empty down the hill.

Amidst the disorder and confusion, it had seemed to be a massive influx, but when all had been housed and counted they numbered less than half the departed population. Uprooted from their homes and their former lives and hopes they were at first as bewildered and distressed as those they had replaced, but soon accepting their fate with patience and resignation they settled to perhaps an unexpected newfound peace.

Gradually the village came to life again. Order was established. A Muchtar was elected and a new custodian appointed to the abbey. The school was reopened. The shops were stocked. Dimitri's coffee shop and the Tree of Idleness once again drew customers, though many fewer than before. The natural village sounds, from houses, streets and gardens and from the hillside where shepherds scrambled with their flocks, began slowly to return. Outwardly, the pattern of daily life is in many ways much the same as it used to be, long years ago before the advent of the tourists, the military occupation and the exodus.

In the mornings the square is emptier, but old men sit there still, sipping coffee, warming themselves in the early sunshine. The younger men go to their work as masons, builders, artisans within the village, or to offices in Kyrenia. Some few cultivate the fields and orchards to which they were not born, and so perhaps with less devotion. The women keep mostly to their houses in old tradition, or tend newly opened shops. Children run or dawdle as ever to the school.

Late in the afternoons the square begins to fill as the men return from work to gather and discuss the doings of the day. Women emerge from their houses and sit outside their doors to chat with neighbours and greet their children drifting home from school. In the evenings, figures appear as before on the hillside paths, carrying baskets and loaves of bread up to their houses. Lights shine through windows for a little while, then one by one they vanish as the village sleeps, lulled by the Skops owls calling and hunting in the stillness of the night.

The clarion bell, once the clock and herald of the village, chiming for the passage of the days, pealing for seasonal festivities, and only sometimes tolling to tell of natural deaths, alas is heard no more. But the abbey as it has for centuries, tells the time of day and the seasons of the year by the changing light and shadows on its walls, the light and shadows which have lately chequered the village and the lives of its changing villagers.

There is no light without its shadow, and no shadow without light. After the most violent disturbances of recent times in the long and troubled history of the island, the light of peace has returned to the little village self-seeded round its parent plant, the Abbaye de la Belle Paix.

The bell, the heart and the voice of the village, hangs still and silent in the belfry. But Bellapais which subdues all enmity within its beckoning embrace, though silent now, still casts its ancient spell upon all who dwell in it.

John and Vivian M. Guthrie
25/9/85.

JOHN GUTHRIE

ABOUT THE AUTHOR

Author and composer Dr John Guthrie (1912-1986), was born in Christchurch, New Zealand. After studying medicine in Scotland at the University of Edinburgh, he moved to Kuwait and was appointed Chief Medical Officer of the Kuwait Oil Company in 1947. During his time in Scotland he met and married Vivian Duncan, daughter of the artist John Duncan. Their daughter Deirdre was born in Scotland in 1941. He founded the first permanent modern hospital in Kuwait in cooperation with the Kuwait State Medical Service. The "Southwell Hospital" was ready for occupation in 1960. In 1962 he retired from medical service and the family moved to Bellapais on the island of Cyprus. There he composed numerous classical pieces for piano forte (among others: The Tinker And The Waterhorse, Spring Tide, Despedida and Cokkils).

JOHN GUTHRIE

A BELL IN BELLAPAIS